Sociology
AND
Public Policy

Sociology
AND
Public Policy

The Case of
Presidential Commissions

Edited by **MIRRA KOMAROVSKY**

ELSEVIER

New York / Oxford / Amsterdam

Elsevier Scientific Publishing Company, Inc.
52 Vanderbilt Avenue, New York, N.Y. 10017

Elsevier Scientific Publishing Company
335 Jan Van Galenstraat, P.O. Box 211
Amsterdam, The Netherlands

Library of Congress Cataloging in Publication Data

Main entry under title:

Sociology and public policy.

1.   Social sciences and state—United States—
Addresses, essays, lectures.   2.   Executive advisory
bodies—United States—Case studies. I. Komarovsky,
Mirra, 1906–
HN65.S582   309.1'73   75-8321
ISBN 0-444-99015-1

Manufactured in the United States of America

Designed by Creative Book Services

CONTENTS

"Come Back When You Can Reach The Conclusions We Want"

—from *Herblock's State Of The Union* (Simon & Schuster, 1972)

ACKNOWLEDGEMENTS

The editor wishes to express her gratitude to Otto N. Larsen, Executive Officer and Alice F. Myers, Administrative Officer of the American Sociological Association for their knowledgeable and efficient help in the organization of the 1973 Plenary Sessions, which led to this publication.

William Gum of Elsevier gave expert and generous help in the preparation of this volume.

INTRODUCTION

MIRRA KOMAROVSKY
Barnard College, Columbia University

The image of a science that could be put to use to improve the world was present in sociology since its inception. Whether a contemporary sociologist chooses to trace his ancestry to Comte, St. Simon, Marx, Durkheim, or other theorists—the founding fathers all shared the heady idea that the new science would provide a guide to public policy. In the ensuing history, however, and under conditions that remain to be specified, the problem of applied social science either receded from or advanced to the forefront of sociological concern. It reemerged in various guises as *Knowledge for What?*, *The Uses of Sociology*, *Sociology in Action*, *Social Theory and Social Practice*, *Applied Sociology: Opportunities and Problems*, and the like.[1]

In my capacity as President of the American Sociological Association, in 1973, I proposed to the Program Committee that two plenary sessions of the Annual Meeting be devoted to that perennial issue of applied sociology—this time, however, to be examined in a concrete and specific context. The plan called for four sociologists who had recently served on Presidential Commissions to reflect upon their experiences in a systematic way. Following the "case studies" by the participants, the second

---

[1]For a review of the literature on applied sociology, see Paul F. Lazarsfeld, Jeffrey G. Reitz, Ann Pasanella. *An Introduction to Applied Sociology* (New York: American Elsevier, 1975).

plenary session was to feature papers, which would attempt to codify the case studies and derive from them, whenever possible, generalizations of a higher order. The proposal was unanimously accepted and this volume represents the final outcome.[2]

My original interest in the plan stemmed from the conviction that in applied science, no less than in basic science, there is no substitute for an empirical study of the phenomenon in question. The participation of a sociologist in a Presidential Commission provides, to be sure, only one of a great variety of natural laboratories in which sociologists attempt to link their discipline to public policy. Microcosm though it be, it was bound to reflect some general problems involved in uses, nonuses, and misuses of sociology.

If the four case histories of Presidential Commissions, however, were to yield any generalizations, some comparability of original descriptions had to be ensured. On the other hand, too rigid an initial schema might foreclose a promising avenue of reflection. The outline (see Appendix) sent to the four Commissioners was intended to eschew both extremes. I suggested a "natural history" approach, following the temporal order of events from *I. The Establishment of the Commission* to *VII. The Aftermath–The Immediate and the Long-Range Effects of the Commission.* Within this frame, and under each of the seven headings, the outline listed a variety of questions and hypotheses intended to alert the four analysts to a common core of theoretical issues. For example, Part IV of the outline asked the four analysts to trace any transformation that may have taken place in the stated objectives of the Commission. Was the original charge so narrowly formulated as to force the participants into the role of technicians expected merely to implement or buttress a predetermined policy?[3] At the other extreme, was the original mandate stated so broadly that the first task of the Commission was to find a focus? If the initial charge did undergo substantial modifications, what were the influences at work? Which constituencies within the Commission, which directives or pressure groups from outside, which contingencies (e.g., a

---

[2]Suggestive monographs in the otherwise meager literature on Presidential Commissions are Frank Popper, *The President's Commissions* (New York: Twentieth Century Fund, 1970) and Urban American Inc. and The Urban Coalition. *One Year Later: An Assessment of the Nation's Response to the Crisis Described by the National Advisory Commission on Civil Disorders* (New York: Frederick Praeger, 1969).

[3]See Robert K. Merton. *Social Theory and Social Structure* (New York: The Free Press, 1968), 267 ff.

premature leak to Congress or to the mass media) played a part in the reformulation of the original mandate?

Another example of the outline may be provided by *Part II. The Collectivities Involved in the Commission, an Organizational Analysis*. This set of probes dealt with the organizational features of the Commission and their consequences for the final recommendations. Having enumerated the separate collectivities, such as the Commissioners, the Administrative Staff, the Research Staff, the use of Task Forces, Consultants, Witnesses, Presidential Representatives, and others, the analysts were to consider the methods of recruitment of each and the possible consequences of such selection of personnel. The relationship of the composition of the Commission to the final outcome presents an important theoretical question. To cite one hypothesis, if the composition is bipartisan and bicameral (Senate and House) with representatives of various interest groups, the pressure for consensus may result in inoffensive but trivial recommendations. Which groups relevant to the purposes of the given Commission were over- and underrepresented? And, again, how did this selectivity bear upon the recommendations?

Another set of questions was focused upon some probable conflicts and modes of their resolution. For example, problems of communication between different professionals, between policy-makers and intellectuals have been the theme of Robert K. Merton's repeated concern.[4] There are other potential conflicts. For example, various government agencies may perceive debated recommendations of the Commission to be threatening or beneficial to themselves. In such situations competing agencies may attempt to win over constituences within the Commission for their respective and conflicting version of recommendations.

We asked the analysts to take cognizance in this organizational analysis of other groups outside the Commission, which may have, in the manner of the competing government agencies, affected the course of its work: the White House, various pressure groups (or the significance of the lack of some organized pressure group), mass media, and the like.[5]

Another section of the outline dealt with cognitive aspects of applied

---

[4]Ibid. 261–278. See also Robert K. Merton. *The Sociology of Science*. (Chicago: The University of Chicago Press, 1973), 70–98.

[5]For the discussion of conflicts generated in one Commission, see Jerome H. Skolnick, "Violence Commission Violence" in *Transaction* Vol. 7, No. 12, October 1970, 31–38. Note also the further documentation of these conflicts in the chapter by Lazarsfeld and Jaeckel, Part Two, in the present volume.

social science. An attempt was made to distinguish various kinds of knowledge which can conceivably form the basis of effective policy. One might begin with a kind of process that is not usually incorporated in the phrase "applied social science"; it is more likely to be termed a "wise administrative judgment." This involves an intuitive assessment of relevant variables, sensitivity to "what the traffic will bear" with regard to a given innovation, and what the further consequences are likely to be. Occasionally, such a creative assessment results in an effective social invention, alleviating a social problem. Even when this assessment is informed by the sociological imagination, applied social science usually connotes a more explicit, rationalistic link between knowledge and decision-making.[6]

The outline listed other forms of knowledge, varying from a general sociological orientation, an inference from a set of verified general propositions, to research explicitly directed to evaluation of competing policy options.[7]

Because the case studies are limited to American Presidential Commissions, the book forfeits the advantages of a comparative perspective. A similar inquiry into the British Royal Commissions or the Swedish experience would illuminate many of the problems here raised. For example, the sponsorship and accountability, the characteristic composition, and the available resources of comparable commissions in various countries would, no doubt, bear upon the relative impact of the commissions' recommendations.

Such were some of the questions sent to the participants, aimed at ferreting out relevant data. In addition to the editor's outline sent at the outset, the four analysts had the benefit of a memorandum prepared by Paul F. Lazarsfeld, which raised a series of similar and other questions. Both the first outline and Dr. Lazarsfeld's memorandum, for all their emphasis upon specific step-by-step analysis, were intended to evoke ideas and evidence bearing upon larger issues in applied sociology.

Stated in the most general way, the barriers to greater utilization of

[6]For emphasis on the distinction between pure and applied social science, see Bernard Berelson, "Sociology in Action: In Population and in General" in Arthur R. Shostak, ed. *Sociology in Action* (Homewood, Ill.: The Dorsey Press, 1966), 15–21.

[7]For a somewhat different classification of types of knowledge relevant to social policy, see Alice M. Rivlin. *Systematic Thinking for Social Action* (Washington D.C.: The Brookings Institute, 1971).

sociology in public policy are cognitive, organizational, and ideological-political.

The interplay between basic and applied sociology is complex. A direct application of some sociological generalization to public policy is likely to be a rare exception and not the rule. The cognitive reasons for the gap between basic and applied social science are manifold. For one thing, the very level of abstraction that makes a single discipline a manageable field of study attenuates its applicability to decision-making. Every discipline selects, through its set of distinctive concepts, certain aspects of reality at the expense of others. Its generalizations therefore always contain the caveat, "other things being equal." For example, Keynesian theory posits a set of determinate relations between a small number of economic aggregates, making the assumption that in the short run, other relevant factors are stable. The theory provided a new way of thinking about economic phenomena and even offered prescriptions as to what to do in order to shift the course of the economy in a desired direction. But Keynesian theory was not any more capable than any other macroeconomic theory of making predictions in a rapidly changing world. The extrapolations on the basis of the theory did not prove accurate enough to provide his followers with an indisputable scientific warrant for their economic programs.[8]

Apart from its high level of abstraction, the cognitive stance of basic sociology is the causal quest, however we define it. It is addressed to the discovery of how the phenomena in its domain are interrelated. But the applied scientist (as several writers have pointed out) must seek out those independent variables that are amenable to control. Since his aim is intervention, he may, recognizing that some potent independent variable is inaccessible to modification, emphasize manipulative variables. Finally, since social problems cut across various disciplines, an applied scientist must be more broadly trained and prepared for interdisciplinary cooperation.

In short, the body of basic science is not likely to address itself to the questions that an applied scientist is called upon to answer, certainly not in a specific enough manner. Even when an inference from the exist-

[8]For a more extended discussion, see William S. Vickery, "Keynesian Theory and Empirical Inquiry" in Mirra Komarovsky, ed. *Common Frontiers of the Social Sciences* (Glencoe, Ill.: The Free Press, 1957), 376–383.

ing knowledge appears to provide the sociological consultant with a ready guide to policy, this insight will probably require empirical validation in the concrete context of the problem in question. One surmises that the sociological consultant could, as an inference from existing theories, more frequently perceive the futility of some proposed solution than be able to supply an effective one. In any event, formulation of policies to cope with social problems will generally require some new research addressed specifically to the question at issue. The sociological perspective and existing sociological generalizations will inform the design of this applied research.

Organizational obstacles in applied social science were illustrated with excerpts from the outline on page 3.

Ideological and political elements are interwoven with cognitive ones at every stage of applied social science. Even the formulation of a problem to be remedied reflects assumptions about the "frozen," not to be questioned, factors. At one extreme, this may take the form of identifying "the problem" with a symptom of a potentially modifiable social condition, in the vain hope that the symptom can be surgically removed from the condition that has bred it and will inevitably breed it again. At the other extreme, some revolutionary formulation of the problem will challenge the basic institutions of a society. Turning from the formulation of the problem to suggested recommendations, we again encounter political aspects. It is difficult to imagine a proposed set of remedies for a major social problem which, whatever their benefits, would not entail costs to some group in prestige, power, or injury to its values. Those adversely affected by a proposed solution may, if informed in time, attempt to mobilize whatever political power they possess to denounce the solution and to urge an alternative, with costs to be borne by some other group. Politically powerful strata might suppress recommendations which they perceive as threatening to themselves, no matter how firmly grounded in knowledge these proposals are.

Valid as the above description of the interpenetration of ideological and cognitive components is, the pessimism it conveys is, no doubt, too stark. A degree of consensus about social problems does exist. It is useful, also, to realize how frequently the debates that rage over public policies, whatever the real interests of the participants, are ostensibly debates over means to common ends. Reliable research may demonstrate the futility of existing programs and show some accepted verities to be based upon myths. Self-interest, masquerading as concern for public welfare, may be unmasked by social science. Similarly, research may make manifest the deleterious consequences of existing social arrangements or values, requiring a reassessment of established institutions. The extent to which these possibilities will be realized depends upon manifold conditions. The state of the social sciences is, obviously, one such condition, affected as it is in a circular manner by the recognition accorded social sciences in a given society and, consequently, the resources made available for their development. The more a society values cognitive rationality in social as well as physical realms, the more open the dissemination of scientific findings, the less concentrated the distribution of political power, the greater would be the strain toward consistency between social science and public policy.[9]

Since the consequences of alternative programs for social behavior are likely to have to be estimated in probabalistic terms, an area of indeterminancy will always remain and continue to constitute an arena of political conflict. By the same token, given favorable societal features and the further development of sociology, we might expect the contribution of sociology to public policy to become more significant. One suspects that all the contributors to this volume, however discouraging they may have found some particular encounter with applied sociology, sustain this ultimate hope.

[9]For an extended discussion of preconditions for applied social science, see Amitai W. Etzioni. *The Active Society* (New York: The Free Press, 1968).

PART ONE

THE CASE HISTORY

CHAPTER ONE

The Commission on Obscenity and Pornography
Form, Function, and Failure

OTTO N. LARSEN

Executive Officer, American Sociological Association

INITIAL RESPONSE: REBUFF AND REBUKE

The Commission on Obscenity and Pornography was conceived in the Congress, born in the White House, and after twenty-seven months of life, was buried without honor by both parent institutions. Now, three years later, it is clear that the third branch of the federal government is not interested in resurrection. In its recent rulings on obscenity, the Supreme Court apparently managed to bypass the work of the Commission. Indeed, the Court has made it less likely that such work will penetrate future policies and influence control procedures.

In effect, then, a serious social and behavioral science research effort has been deemed irrelevant for national policies in this area. The work was denounced by Congress as "irresponsible" and "degrading"; rejected as "morally bankrupt" by President Nixon.

It is not known whether these reactions were generated with or without benefit of exposure to any or all of the 3250 pages of information that the Commission produced and reported in one general report and nine technical volumes available in the U.S. Government Printing Office. It is known that 109 people contributed directly to these reports that recorded in detail 68 separate studies and cost the taxpayers $1,743,000.

It can also be established that the Commission on Obscenity and Pornography, on all its levels, had more input from sociologists and other social scientists than any other commission in government history. Thus, we have what appears to be a clear-cut case of the failure of a social science effort to influence government policy. Or, phrased differently, perhaps we have a classic instance of a "boomerang effect." Thus far, on the federal level at least, the research-oriented report of the Commission appears to have had the opposite impact of that intended by the majority: facts have not stilled fears, laws are more likely to be added than repealed, and there is now more rather than less resistance to the idea that empirical research on the effects of exposure to explicit sex materials is relevant for legislation or for judicial rulings.

Could it have been otherwise? Is emprical inquiry bound to be rebuffed and rebuked in this kind of policy arena? To provide a basis for a response to such questions, we need to know something of the origins, the structure, and the operations of the Commission. This chapter's report will be from the perspective of a sociologist who participated as a Commissioner in the enterprise.

CREATING THE COMMISSION: EFFECT STUDIES AS A CATALYST

The Commission on Obscenity and Pornography, unlike some other well-publicized commissions, was not created in response to an immediate crisis, such as an assassination or civil disorder. Neither was it because a President wished to mobilize support for programs, show concern about a problem, gain new policy ideas, or launch an educational effort. To the contrary, President Johnson was a reluctant participant in the forming of the Commission.

The creation of the Commission was, rather, an attempt by Congress to do something about an irritant that had divided it and had frustrated legislative action for some time. The irritant was the problem of pornography—the emotion it generated and the pressures that it brought on Congress from many sources.[1] But there was agony over the proposed solutions as well. Even the idea of a commission was something of an irritant. In several sessions the Senate passed bills authorizing a commission—but they died in committees of the House. Finally, a concern with effects became the catalyst for decision. Somehow, "libertarian" views, drawing on social science thinking, led to the final act of creating the Commission. This fact merits a brief review of the process.

For a number of years, going back at least to the Gathings Committee in 1952, there had been an almost unbroken succession of hearings before various groups in Congress in which concern about obscenity and pornography was expressed. Mail from constituents and pressure from citizen groups also brought complaints about the "rising tide of smut." In part, the freer flow of what was deemed pornography grew out of the confusion surrounding established law regarding explicit sex material. True, in the 1957 *Roth* case, the Supreme Court had ruled directly for the first time that obscenity was *not* within the area of constitutionally protected speech or press. However, in the litigation that followed over the meaning and application of the standard for determing what is "obscene," ambiguity led to uncertainity, which seemed to promote entrepreneurship in the distribution of sex materials. Congress was thus caught in a cross fire between constitutional uncertainty and complaints from constituents. Civil libertarians and moral authoritarians were in a legislative deadlock. As Senator Karl Mundt said, "It seems to me we are facing up to the alternative of using the commission approach or doing nothing."

In October 1967, Congress passed Public Law 90–100 to establish the Commission on Obscenity and Pornography. It was a remarkable mandate for research that had evolved over five years of processing various

[1] The legal, literary, medical, and social literature is littered with efforts to come to terms with the meaning of pornography. Jurists and journalists, doctors of medicine and divinity, sociologists and semanticists, and psychiatrists and postal officials have labored to bring precision to this troublesome term as well as to such allied concepts as "obscenity," "patently offensive," "hard core," and "prurient." So meticulous have been these definitional pursuits that D. H. Lawrence once referred to them as involving "the splitting of pubic hairs." So unsatisfying and inconclusive have been the results that many are willing to abandon the task and join with Associate Justice Stewart, who once declared that although he could not define "hard-core pornography," he knew it when he saw it.

commission proposals. The emphasis of earlier efforts is reflected in bills that were offered under the following titles: "Commission for the Elimination of Lewd and Obscene Materials," or "The Commission for the Elimination of Pornographic Materials," or the "Establishment of a Commission on Noxious and Obscene Matters and Materials." Such proposals were not without reference to research. Studies were to be undertaken by the Department of Justice, the Post Office, and the Bureau of Customs to find means of "eradication," "suppression," and "prosecution." These bills died in committee; the sentiments behind them did not.

For a congressional consensus to be reached about the Commission, the widespread sentiment for the suppression of obscenity had to be tempered by other considerations. Although no politician is or can appear to be in favor of "smut," some were skeptical about the control options being considered and wanted new information. The break toward agreement came when the question of "effects" was introduced into the deliberations. The idea of scientific evidence was embraced. Nothing was said in these discussions that implied anything other than that such evidence would surely show that obscenity had ill effects. At this point, Senator Mundt, a key figure in the drive to control obscenity, added that ". . . a great deal of work has been done by sociologists and others in this field, and I would hope that with adequate staffing the Commission could come up with a consensus of the findings on this problem."

In the final stages of decision-making, Congress thus transformed its conception of a commission. In early 1967, a bill before the Senate made no mention of effects studies and prescribed that Commissioners should be drawn from both houses of Congress, various government agencies, education, the media, state attorneys general, prosecutors, and law enforcement personnel. It provided for public hearings and power of subpoena.

The Act that ultimately passed the Congress called for effects studies, drew heavily from the behavioral sciences for Commission membership, and removed the power of subpoena.

By including effects in their concern, Congress was able to create the Commission. It was a fateful step. There were dramatic repercussions both throughout and beyond the life of the Commission. The fundamental question was and remains: Is knowledge about the effects of exposure to explicit sex material relevant for making decisions about the forms of control that a society might exercise over obscenity?[2]

In creating the Commission, the Congress seemed to answer this question in the affirmative. This shaped the mandate, depoliticized (to some degree) the selection of the Commissioners, influenced the hiring of staff, gave direction to their work, promoted dissension among Commissioners, affected majority recommendations, stimulated the dissent of the minority, and flavored the reception of the report, whether by friendly or hostile readers.

By including the study of effects in the structure of the Commission, Congress also departed from precedents set in the interpretation of obscenity law. In the landmark *Roth* decision of 1957, the Supreme Court held that the protections of the First and Fourteenth Amendments, with their requirement that harm or an immediate danger of harm be shown in justification of a governmental prohibition, do *not* apply to the dissemination of the "obscene." In one of the 1973 obscenity rulings, the Court stated that effects can be *assumed* and need not be proven by scientific inquiry. It is therefore now permissible for legislatures to act against obscenity on the basis of unprovable assumptions concerning effects. This is quite a different approach from that taken by Congress in creating the Commission, and it certainly was not the principle that guided the Commission in carrying out the mandate of the law under which it worked.

The relevant excerpts from majority opinions, written by Chief Justice Warren Burger, are as follows:

> But it is argued, there is no scientific data which conclusively demonstrates that exposure to obscene materials adversely affects men and women or their society. It is urged on behalf of the petitioner that, absent such a demonstration, any kind of state regulation is "impermissible."

[2]Serious scholars often respond in the negative. James Q. Wilson, for example, concludes a thoughtful analysis with this observation;

In the cases of violence and obscenity, it is unlikely that social science can either show harmful effects or prove that there are no harmful effects. It is unlikely, in short, that considerations of utility or disutility can be governing. These are moral issues, and ultimately all judgments about the acceptability of restrictions on various media will have to rest on political and philosophical considerations (James Q. Wilson, "Violence, Pornography, and Social Science," *The Public Interest*, 22 Winter 1971, p. 61)

We regret this argument. Although there is no conclusive proof of a connection between antisocial behavior and obscene material, the legislature of Georgia could quite reasonably determine that such a connection does or might exist.

From the beginning of civilized societies legislatures and judges have acted on various unprovable assumptions. Such assumptions underlie much lawful state regulation of commercial and business affairs.

If we accept the unprovable assumption that a complete education requires certain books, and the well nigh universal belief that good books, plays, and art lift the spirit, improve the mind, enrich the human personality and develop character, can we then say that a state legislature may not act on the corollary assumption that commerce in obscene books, or public exhibitions focused on obscene conduct, have a tendency to exert a corrupting and debasing impact leading to antisocial behavior?[3]

THE MANDATE: EFFECTS AND CONTROL

Congress, in Public Law 90–100, stated the purpose, assigned four specific duties to the Commission, outlined the resources for use, directed the President to appoint Commissioners according to stated criteria, and called for the Commission to report to the President and to the Congress as soon as practicable, but within two years.

Section One of the three-page Act that became law opened as follows:

> The Congress finds that the traffic in obscenity and pornography is a matter of national concern. The problem, however, is not one which can be solved at any one level of government. The Federal government has the responsibility to investigate the gravity of this situation and to determine whether such materials are harmful to the public, and particularly to minors, and whether more effective methods should be devised to control the transmission of such materials.

The statement then proceeds to note the establishment of an advisory commission whose purpose shall be "*after* a thorough study which shall

---

[3]*The New York Times*, June 22, 1973, p. 42–C.

include a study of the *causal relationship* of such materials to antisocial behavior, to recommend advisable, appropriate, effective, and constitutional means to deal effectively with such traffic in obscenity and pornography." [italics mine]

The law then specifies four duties:

1. With the aid of leading constitutional law authorities, to analyze the laws pertaining to the control of obscenity and pornography; and to evaluate and recommend definitions of obscenity and pornography;

2. To ascertain the methods employed in the distribution of obscene and pornographic materials and to explore the nature and volume of traffic in such materials;

3. To study the effect of obscenity and pornography upon the public, and particularly minors, and its relationship to crime and other antisocial behavior; and

4. To recommend such legislative, administrative, or other advisable and appropriate action as the Commission deems necessary to regulate effectively the flow of such traffic, without in any way interfering with constitutional rights.

The law also authorized the Commission to "make contracts with universities, research institutions, foundations, laboratories, hospitals, and other competent public or private agencies to conduct research on the causal relationship of obscene material and antisocial behavior."

The statements of purpose and specification of duties were often referred to throughout the life of the Commission, but particularly in the research planning stage and in the closing period when recommendations were formulated.

In general, there was substantial agreement on the implications of the mandate. However, the emphasis on effect was a constant thorn in the sides of a few Commissioners. Despite their ardent advocacy of the "rule of law" to protect the social interest in order and morality, these Commissioners seemed to want to depart from the specifications of Public Law 90–100. This is reflected in a minority report issued by two Commissioners and concurred with by a third. These dissents read:

The Commission has deliberately and carefully avoided coming to grips with the basic underlying issue. The government interest in regulating pornography has always related primarily to the prevention of moral corruption and *not* to prevention of overt criminal acts and conduct, or the protection of persons from being shocked and/or offended.

We believe it is impossible, and totally unnecessary, to attempt to prove or disprove a cause-effect relationship between pornography and criminal behavior.[4]

Even though he concurred with the above statements, one Commissioner added the following concern to his separate minority report:

The mandate of Congress was not simply to study the "effect" of obscenity upon the public and minors, but more complete: ". . . to study the effect of obscenity and pornography upon the public, and particularly minors, *and its relationship to crime and other antisocial behavior. . . .*"

I read the "relationship" study as being at least co-equal with the "effect" study. Further, I do not read this duty to study "the relationship (of obscenity) to crime and other antisocial behavior" to be construed so narrow as to require a "direct" cause-effect relationship. For example, in one case of a rape of a 12-year-old girl by a 20-year-old boy, a girlie magazine belonging to the suspect was left at the scene of the attack and was identified by the victim as being in the youth's presence at the time of the attack. The presence of the girlie magazine in the possession of the rapist at the time of the attack is sufficient to warrant notice as a statistic giving evidence of the "relationship" of obscenity to antisocial behavior and bearing on the "rationality" of such legislation.[5]

The dissent then goes on to quote J. Edgar Hoover and other law enforcement officials who have or would provide further illustrations of the kind cited for the type of study that this Commissioner wanted done. The dis-

[4]Commissioners Hill, Link, and C. Keating, *The Report of the Commission on Obscenity and Pornography* (Washington, D.C.: U. S. Government Printing Office, 1970) pp. 383–509.

[5]Commissioner C. Keating, *The Report of the Commission*, p. 562.

senting Commissioner also claimed that when he submitted a memorandum to the Commission calling for such a study, it was ignored. As a point of fact, it was not. A careful analysis of his proposal was made. Included were elementary statements about evidence, proof, and inference in social science. The critique drew heavily from Samuel Stouffer's brilliant 1950 paper on "Some Observations on Study Design," which included the following phrase sharply pinpointing the problem with the Commissioner's proposal: "Sometimes, believe it or not, we have only one cell." Incidentally, Commissioner Keating did not ignore sociologists altogether. In his minority report he quotes Pitirim Sorokin as follows: ". . . there is no example of a community which has retained its high position on the cultural scale after less rigorous sexual customs have replaced more restricting ones."

Another section of the mandate also drew some fire. Commissioner Keating reported that he could not find warrant in the mandate for the Commission's efforts to explore what came to be known as "positive approaches" to obscenity control. The Commission's decision to pursue such approaches involved an interpretation of point four in the duties enumerated by the Act, which called for recommendations of "such legislative, administrative, or other advisable and appropriate" controls. The interpretation that led to some exploration of nonlegislative action was directly traceable to the social scientists on the Commission.

However, on this Commission and, I suspect, on many others, the conceptual, research, and interpretive effort required in this area is formidable. It takes concerted effort to convince Commissioners, let alone policy-makers, that policy is not necessarily synonymous with law, or that social control can mean anything other than law enforcement. Tradition, government sponsorship, and the usual mix of commissioners make for a heavy commitment to the legal approach. Social research can be relevant to social policy in this context, but, for sociologists, too often this may mean little more than being technocrats to serve predetermined ends. One staff sociologist from the Commission on Obscenity and Pornography (Weldon Johnson) concluded that we had not been very effective in posing the central question regarding the wisdom of law, which is: What *laws* with what *sanctions* have what *consequences* for society in its attempt to establish desired *conduct?*

THE COMMISSIONERS: HOT POTATOES IN A NO WIN GAME

Elizabeth Drew once described participation on Presidential Commissions as "self-inflicted hotfoots." Before this glow can occur, an act of appointment must take place.

Three months after Congress authorized the Commission, President Johnson, in a terse statement, announced the appointment of eighteen Commissioners of obscenity and pornography. The roster of names and affiliations seemed to indicate that the President was sensitive to the guidelines stated in the law, which required that the members "shall include persons having expert knowledge in the fields of obscenity and antisocial behavior, including but not limited to psychiatrists, sociologists, psychologists, criminologists, jurists, lawyers, and others from organizations and professions who have special and practical competence or experience with respect to obscenity laws and their application to juveniles."[6]

It is difficult to find out precisely how the material was processed in the White House to enable the President to make the appointments to the Commission. I have recently learned from President Johnson's then top personnel advisor that the President would never have created the Commission on his own initiative. When confronted with the task of appointment, the President's attitude was characterized by the phrase, "This is a hot potato in a no win game." It is also interesting to recall that although the appointments were made in January 1968, the Commission was delayed until its funding was authorized six months later. Between those two dates, President Johnson made his dramatic announcement that he would not seek another term in office. In contrast to his approach to the Violence Commission, at no point before his term expired in Jan-

[6]Just before final passage of the law, Senator Mundt was successful in adding, by amendment, the following words contained in this section: "from organizations and professions," "and practical," "or experience." Whether or not this was a last minute effort to try to ensure that representatives from groups who had been agitating for more obscenity controls could be appointed to the Commission, Commissioner Charles Keating, who is also the founder of the Citizens for Decent Literature, does imply this in his minority report, where he criticizes the emphasis given to the study of effects by social scientists and states that the Mundt Amendment indicates that "it was the clear intent of Congress that practical experience was to play a substantial role in this entire investigation . . ." (*The Report of the Commission*, p. 561. Also, on p. 529 Commissioner Keating lists the "Honorary Committee Members" of Citizens for Decent Literature, Inc. Eleven U. S. Senators are named, including Senator Mundt.)

uary 1969, did the President or any of his representatives request any information from the Commission on Obscenity and Pornography. The White House talent hunt for this Commission, as it was described to me both at the time of my appointment and recently by the advisor involved, was more of a problem of omissions from the Commission than anything else.[7] The hot potato had to be cooled. This meant fending off requests from several organizations that desperately wanted representation. A member of the Washington bureau of the *Los Angeles Times* described one such incident in the following way:[8]

> When the Commission was first established—with Mr. Keating one of the prime lobbyists for it before Congress—his friends worked hard to get President Johnson to appoint him. But even the influence of the then Senator Frank J. Lausche (D., Ohio), himself a prominent and outspoken anti-pornographer, was unavailing.

President Johnson did appoint a Keating to the Commission, but not the one mentioned in the quotation above. He appeared later. Johnson's Keating was a former Republican Senator from New York, Kenneth Keating, then a judge. Kenneth Keating resigned from the Commission in June 1969, when President Nixon appointed him Ambassador to India. Nixon then made his only appointment to the Commission, Charles H. Keating, Jr., a Cincinnati lawyer and founder of Citizens for Decent Literature, Inc.

The two Keatings were not related in any fashion. The departure of Kenneth Keating took from the Commission its only national political figure. The arrival of Charles Keating came when the Commission had been under way for one year. Procedures had been adopted, and the re-

[7]When I was called from the White House and asked to serve on the Commission, I pointed out that I had not been involved with any research specifically concerned with obscenity and pornography. I was told that the President was looking for qualified people who had experience with research that would be relevant, but that he did not want persons who had already made up their minds about the subject. I responded by asking if this meant that the Commission was free to move with the data and was not being formed merely to provide information to support a given policy position. The answer was an emphatic yes, and I was given some names of prominent persons who were not being put on the Commission because they had publicly committed themselves to a particular view on the issue. Thereupon, I accepted the appointment.

[8]Jules Witcover, "Commissioners and Zealots: Civil War Over Smut," *The Nation*, May 11, 1970, p. 551.

search program had been initiated. Charles Keating took such exception to the procedures and to the direction of the work that he attended only three sessions of the Commission, each time briefly, during the remaining fifteen months. Even though he chose not to participate in the work and in the deliberations, the final 646-page report of the Commission contained a vigorous 117-page dissent by Keating. In retrospect, his appointment by President Nixon is all the more remarkable because of Keating's general assessment of commissions as contained in his dissent:

> So-called Presidential Commissions do not work. They never will. Such Commissions, in my opinion, are not a valid part of the American political system. The structure of the Commission on Obscenity and Pornography was similar to that of other Commissions. This Commission was not responsible to anyone, either to the President who appointed it, the Congress which created it, or to the people whom the Congress represented.
>
> . . . In the case of the Commission on Obscenity and Pornography, with men such as Jack Valenti and Abe Fortas in key advisory roles in the Johnson Administration, it was more likely than not that the orientation of the Commission for permissiveness would be exactly opposite the orientation intended by Congress; namely, for moral discipline and responsibility . . . .[9]

Keating has perhaps spoken more authoritatively about his own belated appointment as a Commissioner. On this he was quoted in the press as follows: ". . .the White House knew when I was appointed my interest was to control pornography. . . . They didn't send me in as an objective observer."[10]

President Johnson, reluctant as he may have been to enter the arena, did appoint persons to the Commission who could be objective observers. Although it might not have been possible to select without reference to constituencies, Johnson's appointments did not, with one exception, have an apparent vested interest one way or the other in obscenity and pornography. The exception was Father Hill, who came to the Commission from the post of Executive Secretary of Morality in the Media, Inc. This he described in his Commission biography as "the interfaith organization

[9]*Report of the Commission*, pp. 516–517.
[10]*Los Angeles Times*, March 25, 1970.

working to counter the effects of obscene material on the young, and working toward media based on the principles of truth, taste, inspiration, and love."

If the other Commissioners had a pre-existing commitment concerning obscenity and pornography, it perhaps more closely resembled disinterest than anything else. To some extent, Public Law 90–100 required this, and President Johnson made his appointments accordingly.

The result was eighteen Commissioners, sixteen men and two women, who came from fourteen states. Geography and gender are easy to identify. The constituencies that the Commissioners were intended to represent, or did represent, if any, can only be inferred from certain other characteristics. Lawyers, professors, and clergymen were prominent, but there was even overlap in representation from these categories. Thus, for example, one Commissioner was both a professor of broadcast-film art and an ordained Methodist minister.

One third of the Commissioners had law degrees. At the time of appointment, these persons were called from positions as dean of a law school, chief judge of a state juvenile court, judge in a federal court of appeals, attorney for the Motion Picture Association of America (the only nonwhite member of the Commission), businessman in the book and magazine distribution field, and state attorney general.

Four Commissioners were clergymen: one a rabbi, one a Catholic priest from Morality in the Media, one a professor of communications, and one an administrator of a Methodist retirement home.

Three sociologists were appointed to the Commission: two were professors and the third was a director of social research for a television network. Two Commissioners were M.D.s, both psychiatrists, one a professor and the other from the Menninger Foundation. Of the remaining Commissioners, one was a professor of English, one a director of a university library, and one a vice-president of a book publishing company.

In sum, the appointments were mainly male, white, professional persons, none of whom were under forty years of age. A majority held graduate degrees and either were or had been professors or teachers in such fields as law, theology, sociology, criminology, communications, psychiatry, library science, and English. The biographies also indicate that several Commissioners had been presidents of national professional associations, including the Association of American Law Schools, the American

Library Association, the American Orthopsychiatric Association, the American Association for Public Opinion Research, and the American Society of Criminology.

These elements imply that this was to be a Commission tilted toward persons with academic orientations. To be sure, a number of the Commissioners had served on government advisory panels, task forces, and review boards. One person had also been a Commissioner on the President's Commission on Law Enforcement and the Administration of Justice. In addition, one of the sociologist Commissioners, concurrent with the present appointment, was on duty in a high staff position on the Violence Commission. The coincidence of being called to serve both sex and violence simultaneously was a fine tribute to sociology, but it placed great and often irreconcilable demands on one sociologist.

With the Commission thus cast, the scene was set for what one President sensed would be a "no win game" and for what his successor would virtually ensure as a loss by his pietistic politics and by his appointments to the Supreme Court. Yet the loss was not the failure to adopt a particular set of recommendations, or even the harsh criticism of the research procedures and findings. It was, rather, the failure of The Report, for the time being at least, to penentrate the policy realm with the principle that empirical research is relevant.

This, I suspect, the majority of the Commissioners now feel rather deeply. At the outset and during the time of work, we did not know, nor did we seriously try to anticipate, what the political response might be. At every point, when a dissenting Commissioner stated that this was not what the Congress or the President wanted, the Commission, under a chairman who was dedicated to finding facts, kept moving toward those facts. By and large, this kept the proceedings cool. Given the sensitive subject matter, any leap ahead to a discussion of desired controls tended to evoke emotion. The prevailing attitude was that there was work to be done and that, when the information required was obtained, the Commission would sit down and decide what the implications were.

Accordingly, for two years there was a relentless pursuit of data. Policy deliberations came to the surface only in the final two months. Indeed, they were systematically pursued by the entire Commission only over an intensive two-day period in July 1970.

In retrospect, it is astounding to recall how, in its general deliberations, the Commission kept policy implications in abeyance for so long.

Until we met in July 1970, to review the final summation of the research and to formulate recommendations, I did not know, nor could I have predicted, what the majority of the Commission would do about various policy options. As the voting time approached, I shared the feeling, but not the judgment, of one clergyman Commissioner, who said, "I can't believe what I am hearing," as each Commissioner gave testimony reacting to a key proposal concerning the repeal of laws that restricted adult exposure to sex materials.

I mentioned these points at this time, even before reviewing the organization and work of the Commission, because they reflect the strategy of the Commission, which itself was a product of the structure of appointments, the background and experience of the Commissioners, and perhaps the absence of empirical data on obscenity that we found at the outset. But more than that, the state of the social sciences as perceived at that time equipped us to do what was essentially abstracted empirical research; it did not equip us to shape the research around policy alternatives. Policy was something you took up after you had done the research.

This is where we missed a rare opportunity to link social research to social policy in an effective manner. We failed because we did not turn our tools first to an empirical analysis of policy options, so that the remainder of the research on effects and other elements would illuminate the costs and consequences of realistic alternative courses of action. In short, we did not have a policy research theory to guide our strategy.

What the Commission did have was the challenge of meeting the Congressional mandate to perform four duties, a leader who marshaled all our resources for those duties, an enthusiasm for the work, and a short time period to put it all together.

THE CHAIRMAN AND THE SOCIOLOGISTS: COMMITMENT AND RESPONSE TO RESEARCH

In July 1968, the Commission held its first meeting. The site, the Institute for Sex Research at Indiana University, was selected to afford an exposure to the sex-oriented materials available in its extensive archives, alleged to be, after the Vatican, the second largest holding in the world. Beyond that, the purpose of the meeting was to hear expert reviews of the literature and to plan for the organization of the work of the Commission. Several policy decisions were made that were later to raise points of dispute among some of the Commissioners. But first there was the matter of the chairmanship.

Although Public Law 90–100 stipulated that "the Commission shall elect a Chairman and a Vice Chairman from among its members," the White House announcement of appointments identified William Lockhart, dean of the Law School at the University of Minnesota, as chairman. Later, the dissenters saw this as a scheme by the administration to direct the Commission toward preconceived goals of the kind envisaged in the following statement by dissenting Commissioner Charles Keating: ". . . although Professor Lockhart did not pay his current dues to avoid the telltale association, he is and has been, for all practical purposes, a member of the American Civil Liberties Union."[11]

At the first meeting of the Commission, Dean Lockhart was elected chairman, and Professor Frederick Wagman, director of the University of Michigan Library, was elected vice-chairman. Chairman Lockhart, a recognized authority on constitutional law, brought his experience both as a scholar and as a leader in academic, church, and civic affairs immediately to bear on the work of the Commission. The significance of this goes beyond style to the direction of his commitment. Even with social scientists on the Commission, it was unlikely that we could have stayed on an empirical track in the pursuit of the four duties without his reasoned support and vigorous leadership. He resisted all effort to use money for public relations types of activities, in the interest of allocating funds to research. He read every article, research proposal, and report. He even labored on some of the questionnaires. By his example, it became clear that this was to be a working commission, not one that merely reviewed the work of others.

This extraordinary commitment merits further comment. It is not surprising that cleavages occur between lawyers and social scientists, since they are trained in different rules of evidence, and lawyers tend to think about principles rather than data underlying the law. What kept the cleavage under control on this Commission was a lawyer-chairman who was interested in what *empirical* conditions were assumed by various types of legislation. He was not only interested in it, he pressed for research, and the results influenced his policy judgment. The extent of this

[11]*Report of the Commission*, p. 518.

influence was indicated in the following report of an interview that took place shortly after the Commission's work was done:

> Dean Lockhart said that before he undertook the task of heading the commission . . . he had favored control of obscenity for both children and adults. As a result of what he described as "scientific studies of the effects of erotic material" conducted by commission researchers he said he had changed his mind in relation to adults. The evidence was "overwhelming," he said, that such materials do not contribute to antisocial behavior of any sort.[12]

The chairman thus reports that he shifted policy grounds because of the research on effects. How does that compare with the response of the sociologists on the Commission? In general, the sociologists were more cautious in their characterization of the evidence, but more radical in their application of it to policy, at least in two out of three cases. Thus, as a sociologist, I did not find the evidence "overwhelming," but rather convincing, or even compelling. This was strong enough to move me from the neutral ground of an uncommitted predisposition on this subject to a recommendation, shared with Commissioner Wolfgang, that *all* existing statutes on obscenity or pornography should be repealed. This recommendation was made because we honestly believed that the weight of all the evidence supported it, and because we hoped it would counter the conservative dissidents, thereby adding credibility to the majority position.

The potency of the majority policy position—supported by lawyer-Commissioner Lockhart and sociologist-Commissioner Klapper, as well as by ten other of the seventeen participating Commissioners—and the extreme position taken by sociologist-Commissioners Larsen and Wolfgang was characterized by the critic, Stanley Kauffmann, in the following terms:

> September 30, 1970, was a red-letter day in American social history. The majority report of the Federal Commission . . . published that day, is a revolutionary document . . . no one in his right mind would have predicted as recently as 1960 that a federal commission would make such a recommendation only ten years later . . . The Lock-

[12]Susan Wagner, "Porno Report Becomes Political Football," *Publishers' Weekly*, October 12, 1970, p. 34.

hart report and the Larsen-Wolfgang supplement are strong stuff to
come from a Washington podium. In a culture-tradition sense, they are
anti-American . . . it puts the central issue right on the line. The commission does not contend that pornography is desirable but that the law
cannot deal with it satisfactorily. . . . Once those obscurantist and prov-
cative laws are out of the way, there will be more chance for the social
changes already in motion to prosper. . . The Lockhart report is just
possibly epoch-making, and it's an epoch that needs to be made.[13]

Some broader concerns in the linkage of social research to social policy
can perhaps be illuminated from this account of how different degrees of
attitude-shift resulted from the positive appraisals of empirical evidence.
On the surface, at least, effect studies by social scientists had a powerful,
if not an overwhelming, impact on the Commissioners when they finally
made their policy recommendations. However, the "effects" question as
it relates to policy decision-making is more complicated than either the
lawyers or the sociologists appreciated at the time.

Whatever the claim, one cannot and does not make policy judgments
on the basis of effects evidence alone. A set of interlocking questions posing problems of criteria emerge in the process of moving from the data
to the policy recommendations. Apart from the well-known difficulty of
establishing relationships in research, let alone causal relationships, it is
difficult for most people to frame the effects question in this broader context.

For example, assume that research has shown that exposure to sex
material has an effect on X (greater than zero but less than one). Such
a finding raises several interpretive questions that are not ordinarily made
explicit, at least in the press of moving to a conclusion in a commission
context. First: What is the importance/magnitude of the effect *compared
to other things* that also affect X? The problem is that many things, sex-
oriented or otherwise, can have an effect on X. Topics like obscenity, however, tend to get distorted in the dialogue on effects because selective
attention is given to just one independent variable in isolation.

The second question is: How do we feel about these effects? Thus,
if one million people read pornography, and one hundred rapes occur,
how do we feel about that? Or, from other areas, if 60 million people
view "Hijacked" on TV, and six actual hijack attempts follow, how do we

[13]"Stanley Kauffmann on Obscenity," *New Republic*, October 17, 1970, pp. 34–35.

feel about that? If 60 million people drink alcohol and 500,000 auto deaths follow, how do we feel about that? If we were to follow the model of the economists in their analysis of employment, it could be asserted that we cannot tolerate more than 7 percent unemployment. This approach could be used in other problem areas, but empirical evidence does not, in and of itself, provide us the criterion.

The third question is: Given the effect, and given how we feel about it, what level of intervention is justified? This is where principles and competing interests play off against each other. Do the number of rapes that censorship permits us to avoid justify limitations on freedom of speech? Does the decrease in auto accidents made possible by Prohibition justify removing alcohol from everyone?

Sociologists are perhaps best equipped to contribute most to the first two questions: the matter of what the effects are and, through opinion research, the matter of how people feel about them. This was the contribution we attempted and achieved to a considerable extent on this Commission. The third question, which is *the* policy judgment, can be approached and informed equally well from any quarter. Here the sociologist can bring into focus the options and alternatives. This, as I have already noted, we failed to do in any significant way, except perhaps as a parting shot.

ORGANIZING THE WORK: RULES AND PROCEDURES

Four decisions made at the first meeting of the Commission structured the means by which the base of empirical evidence was to be built. These decisions involved (1) hiring the staff, (2) setting norms for communication, (3) delegating responsibilities, and (4) timing the public hearings.

The Staff

The total professional and supporting staff of the Commission barely outnumbered the total number of Commissioners—twenty-two versus eighteen (twelve in professional roles and ten in support capacities).

The staff was headed by an executive director recommended by a committee, Dr. W. Cody Wilson, who had been trained in social psychology at Harvard, had taught at the University of Texas, and had directed contract research in the Department of Defense. He also was to serve as the Commission's director of research. Except for the general counsel, Paul Bender, a professor of law from the University of Pennsylvania,[14] the executive director also appointed the remainder of the staff.

This concentration of authority in the executive and research director was a deliberate decision to facilitate coordination of efforts and, given the director's background, was a further indication of the Commission's commitment to pursue social science research in the performance of its duties. This was also reflected in the qualifications of the professional staff, about one-third of whom were trained in law and two-thirds in the social sciences, including three persons from sociology. Two staff sociologists had received a considerable part of their graduate training under the supervision of two of the Commissioners. These characteristics meant that both the formal and informal relationships between the staff and most of the Commissioners were harmonious and productive.

Confidentiality

Among the important impressions that emerged from the orientations at the first Commisson meeting were: (1) little empirical evidence had been recorded concerning effects and the other problems we were to study; and (2) this was indeed a "sensitive" area and special precautions would be advisable in order to persuade qualified researchers to initiate and complete the contemplated research.

Accordingly, the Commission, acting directly out of this specific concern and without reference to further implications or other possible consequences, adopted a rule of confidentiality. There were other consequences. This approach minimized publicity and helped give the Commission a "low profile" for about a year. However, the policy also came under severe attack in Commissioner Keating's dissent.

[14]The integrity of Professor Bender was also attacked in the separate statements filed by Commissioners Hill, Link, and Keating on the grounds of his membership in the ACLU.
    Professor Bender is a highly qualified legal scholar in the area of obscenity law. Among other experiences, he once served on the government side in the successful prosecution of the Ginzburg case before the Supreme Court. As legal counsel, Bender came to know and appreciate the utility of social science data. He was particularly impressed with the absence of "consensus" in public opinion about the harmful effects of pornography; he did not, however, think of this as a question prior to the Commission's national survey.

The opposing views, an almost classic contrast of purposes and interpretation, can best be seen through brief reference to the record. The problem is one that will persist as researchers work in sensitive areas. First, the official position of the Commission:

> The Commission fully subscribed from the beginning to the Congressional directive to make recommendations only after thorough study. To implement this approach, it was determined that confidentiality by Commission members should be maintained. This was felt to be necessary to encourage maximum exploration and free discussion of opinions, data, and new ideas at meetings of the Commission, to enhance open and unbiased investigations in sensitive areas, to avoid public misinterpretations of research data, and to prevent premature conclusions. Moreover, the Commissioners felt it was important, in order to avoid confusion as to the activities of the Commission to have but one spokesman prior to the completion of its Report.[15]

Commissioner Keating countered in the following fashion:

> One final fact—one final ironical fact. This Commission, the majority of which opted for absolute freedom for the pornographers, is the very same Commission which at its very first meeting imposed upon all its members a cloak of secrecy—a vow of silence. No Commissioner was permitted, outside of the hallowed halls of the Commission meetings, to discuss, give interviews, make public statements, etc., regarding the work of the Commission, the opinions of the Commissioners, etc. My request for admission to the press to the meetings of either the Commission or its Panels was refused. Amazing! Incredible! Beyond belief! The "confidentiality rule" of the Commission is understandable when viewed in the light of the fact that every effort was made by the majority of the Commission to eliminate dissent. As a matter of fact, it was necessary for me to go to Court in order to obtain the right to speak up, the right to dissent.[16]

What Commissioner Keating does not record in this account is that at the last meeting of the Commission, with deadlines looming large, he introduced a motion that the Commission conclude without issuing *any*

[15]*The Report of the Commission*, p. 527.
[16]Ibid.

written reports, and that if this was not complied with, he would go to court to gain time to prepare his lengthy dissent. The motion was defeated. He went to court, but an out-of-court agreement was reached giving him two weeks—the day before the final Commission report was to be released—to prepare and include his 117-page dissent. After an all-night publishing run on presses at the Department of Defense, enough copies of the entire report were produced to release the report on the September 30 deadline to the President and a few members of Congress. Several days later, the Government Printing Office began its output of the document.

Earlier, the Commission's low profile began to rise in the national press. Commissioner Hill broke the confidentiality rule over a Commission-sponsored experimental study and conveyed his outrage to the syndicated columnist, Jack Anderson. The study, conducted by a psychologist and two physicians, was exploring the threshold of satiation. The research marked a first attempt to study the effects of repeated (ninety minutes per day) and prolonged (three weeks) exposure to erotica. It involved volunteer male university students, aged twenty-one to twenty-three. Attitudinal, behavioral, and physiological measures were employed. The latter were deemed particularly offensive.

Confidentiality began to disappear completely toward the end of the Commission's life, as drafts of reports were circulated. On August 11 and 12, 1970, Congressman Robert Nix called the Subcommittee on Postal Operations into session to hear testimony on the forthcoming Commission Report. A non-Commission sociologist appraised the hearings in the following terms:

> Nix's actions were one of the first clearly manifested signs that the Commission Report was being viewed as a politically sensitive document and that there were political points to be made by being one of the first to denounce it. . . . There was a kind of curious semantic acrobatics on the part of many of those who testified, for all were making judgments and evaluations about a report which had not been released. They were essentially relying upon leaked information which one can assume was only selectively leaked.[17]

[17]Ray C. Rist, "The Politics of Pornography: A Study of the Natural History of the Commission on Obscenity and Pornography," unpublished paper, 1973.

Division of Labor

In response to the Congressional mandate, the Commission organized itself into four working panels: a traffic and distribution panel, an effects panel, a positive-approaches panel, and a legal panel. The chairman of the Commission was *ex officio* on each panel. Each panel had its own chairman (the attorney general for traffic, a sociologist for effects, a psychiatrist for positive approaches, and a judge for legal). The three sociologist-Commissioners were concentrated on the effects panel, which had five members, all Ph.D.s. All the other panels had four members. Staff members were also assigned to each panel. For example, two staff sociologists worked on the effects assignment.

Each panel was charged with developing a research plan for its part of the mandate. The specific projects were then to be negotiated, for the most part by the executive and research director.[18] Approximately one million dollars was spent directly on research, with 40 percent going to effects, 25 percent to traffic and distribution, 20 percent to positive approaches, and 15 percent to legal analyses. Each panel received interim papers, processed research, and produced a final report to the Commission covering its area of work. Although there was some liaison between the panels, this structure emphasized specialization of tasks for Commissioners. Communication among sectors was not always satisfactory, mainly because so much research was concentrated into such a brief time span. The Commissioners had a tremendous assignment toward the end, responsible as they were for reading three panel reports besides the one they had worked on. Under this division of labor, two positions gained increasing importance as we moved toward the final stage. The chairman of the Commission and the executive and research director became the most knowledgeable generalists among us. For many of the Commissioners, the entire experience was much like entering an intensive two-year

[18]Embarrassment and negative response were frequently encountered by the director when he first confronted potential researchers. However, curiosity was also present and when it was coupled with funds, resistance was generally overcome. In its report, the effects panel concluded, "One of the contributions of the work . . . has been to place the dimension of human sexual behavior on the agenda for continuing inquiry. By providing resources in terms of funds and technical guidelines, [the Commission] has helped to legitimate inquiry into an area that heretofore has either been ignored or feared. We strongly recommend that such research be further funded and encouraged" (*The Report of the Commission*, p. 140).

research seminar, having a two-week study period, and concluding with
a two-day final exam.

Despite the concentration of sociologists on the effects panel, many
of the thirty-nine studies that this panel used in its final reports were
more from the psychological side of social psychology than from the sociological side. This may have been appropriate, but it was also a function
of the training, interests, and sociometric connections of the executive
and research director, who usually exercised final authority in allocating
grants for research. However, the entire effects panel was deeply involved in every decision in the planning, development, and evaluation
of the competitive bids for the Commission's largest study. This was a
national probability sample survey involving face-to-face interviews with
2486 adults and 769 young persons (ages fifteen to twenty). This study
cost approximately $225,000 and produced data for all the panels. The sur-
vey had three general purposes: (1) to identify the amount, frequency,
and circumstances of the public's exposure to erotic materials; (2) to describe community standards and norms pertaining to distribution, consumption, and control of erotica; and (3) to collect other relevant data
concerning the correlates of exposure to erotic materials.

A few key findings of the national survey may be cited for what they
reveal about effects as a factor in public opinion, which, in turn, had considerable influence, when coupled with experimental and other studies, on
the recommendations of the Commission:

1 When presented with an array of presumed effects, including those classified as "socially desirable," "neither clearly
   socially approved nor disapproved," and "socially undesirable," there was no presumed effects upon which more
   than two-thirds of the adult population agreed. (The most
   widely held opinions, also supported by experimental
   studies, were that erotic materials excite people sexually
   and provide information about sex.)

2 People were generally far more likely to say they had
   personally experienced socially desirable or neutral effects
   than socially undesirable effects. Persons who had envisaged
   undesirable effects rarely or never reported having personally experienced them, and were more likely to say they had

occurred without reference either to themselves or to anyone they personally knew.

3 A majority of American adults (59 percent) believed that adults should be allowed to read or see any explicit sex materials they wanted to.

4 Two-fifths of American adults would change their views about restrictive laws, in one direction or another, on the basis of clear demonstrations that there were or were not harmful effects. Of these, about one-half would be inclined to sanction availability of erotic materials if they felt sure that such materials would have no harmful effects; on the other hand, eight persons in ten would oppose availability of such materials if they were convinced that such materials were harmful.

5 Almost half the population believed that laws against sexual materials would be "impossible to enforce." If restrictive laws were to be passed, 62 percent would rather have federal than state or local legislation.

Research Strategy in the Study of Effects

The Commission's study of effects was generated by congressional intent but, as implied in the survey results above, was reinforced in its importance as the Commission moved farther into its inquiries. A brief outline of how effects were studied follows.

In the execution of its duties, the panel moved successively through standard procedures of social science inquiry. Beginning with conceptualization, concern was directed toward specification of the stimulus and identification of effects. The panel refined the concepts after an inventory of past research and other literature, in which claims had been made about the consequences of reading or viewing erotic materials (thirty-six presumed consequences were identified and classified as harmful, neutral, or helpful). The panel next undertook to formulate a set of seven general research goals, to outline appropriate research designs, and to examine feasible methods of inquiry. A variety of research methods were judged to be potentially responsive to the goals, and a decision was made to employ multiple methods to complement and supplement one another.

Thus, in a variety of settings, using an array of effect indicators, surveys, quasi-experimental studies, studies of rates and incidence at the community level and controlled experimental studies were undertaken to approach the general question: Under what conditions do certain effects take place?

Sensitivity to the experience of earlier commissions and to sex-oriented research in the past induced the panel to be particularly mindful of reporting the limitations in both methods and data. Specific references were also made to major problems remaining for the study of effects, and suggestions were included as to how these might be approached.

Such sensitivity to professional standards did not, and should not, ward off criticism of the research, particularly from scientific sources. Critical reviews from such quarters have just begun to appear. More frequently, what has been registered is the observation that the Commission found "no effects." That is not true. The panel report is replete with findings of physiological, attitudinal, judgmental, and behavioral effects, some commonly anticipated (e.g., arousal), some surprising (e.g., "calloused" sexual attitudes toward women *decreased* immediately after viewing erotic films and continued to decrease up to two weeks later). Many of the effects of exposure to erotica are suggested by simple correlations, but the direction of the relationship is clarified in many cases by reference to controlled experiments.

What the panel did conclude about effects, after analyzing the pattern of results from thirty-nine studies, including fourteen controlled experiments, was summarized in the opening statement to its reports as follows:

> If a case is to be made against "pornography" in 1970, it will have to be made on grounds other than demonstrated effects of a damaging personal or social nature. Emprical research designed to clarify the question has found no reliable evidence to date that exposure to explicit sexual materials plays a significant role in the causation of delinquent or criminal sexual behavior among youth or adults.[19]

This statement itself has had one notable effect: it has become the most widely quoted excerpt from the entire Commission report.

[19]*Report of the Commission*, p. 139.

Public Hearings

From his experience with the Violence Commission, Jerome Skolnick has referred to public hearings as a "form of theater" where "conclusions must be presented to evoke an emotional response in both the commissioners and the wider television audience."[20]

Some members of the Commission on Obscenity and Pornography suggested that public hearings be held at the beginning of the Commission's life. However, perhaps sensing Skolnick's point, the Commission concluded that in the first stage of its work, public hearings would not be a likely source of accurate data or a wise expenditure of its limited resources. The social scientists all concurred in the judgment to delay hearings until data were at hand that could be illuminated in such a forum.

The delay caused strain and tension. Finally, two Commissioners could not tolerate the delay; in February 1970, Commissioners Hill and Link conducted, at their own expense, a series of public hearings in eight cities across the country.[21] Later, in their dissent, they were to describe their witnesses as "a cross-section of the community, ranging from members of the judiciary to members of women's clubs." In New York, this particular cross-section produced twenty-six out of twenty-seven witnesses who "expressed concern and asked for remedial measures." From their hearings, they concluded "that the majority of American people favor tighter controls." They used these impressions to counter the conclusions of the Commission's national survey.

In May 1970, the full Commission held four days of public hearings. Twenty-eight witnesses were heard in Los Angeles and thirty were heard in Washington D.C. Representatives from diverse organizations were present in both instances. In Los Angeles, for example, these included the mayor, a movie star, a police captain, a judge, and persons representing such groups as Planned Parenthood, the American Library Association, Citizens for Decent Literature, National Council of Teachers of English, and Christians and Jews for Law and Morality.

The hearings in Washington were similar in representation and argu-

[20]Jerome H. Skolnick, "Violence Commission Violence," *Transaction* October 1970. p. 36.

[21]*Report of the Commission*, p. 387.

ment. Point and counterpoint were made. Both sides were earnest in their counsel to the Commission, and both appeared hopeful that the Report, still five months away, would support their positions. For the Commission, the four-day forum was at least an interesting review of arguments, all of which had been revealed in reviews of the literature or in earlier discussions.

These four days would have passed by largely unnoticed by the public had it not been for an unusual incident that occurred toward the end of the last day. The incident merits brief reference only because its novelty provoked an instant worldwide mass-media response. From that day forward, the Commission lost its treasured anonymity.

It is not my purpose to suggest that "Obscenity is as American as cheese pie," but merely to note that the thought occurred to me on the afternoon of May 13, 1970, in the New Senate Office Building when Thomas King Forcade, coordinator of the Underground Press Syndicate and self-styled "self-ordained minister of the Church of Life," concluded his testimony before the Commission by pushing such a pie in my face.

The pie-throwing incident was dramatic for many reasons. To be sure, it violated the dignity and decorum of an official hearing. But it also had a stronger offensive intent; in a setting where the subject was how we shall or shall not communicate about sex, the incident that followed Forcade's testimony rudely broke through the boundaries set for the "proper" discussion of that topic, even when the limits are stretched to accommodate the rawest reach of pornography. Five times Mr. Forcade ended paragraphs about "witchhunts" and "McCarthy-like hearings" in his prepared statement with a ringing, "Fuck off, and fuck censorship!" And one point in his testimony, during a curious silent spell, a three-year old girl accompanying Forcade's forces came toward the podium and echoed the first half of his refrain. Not even the First Amendment lawyers on the Commission were equipped by precedent to respond to that outburst.

The pie came in response to my question challenging his allegations about "McCarthy-like" procedures. I resisted the temptation to respond either in kind (a pie was available) or with some other force. Midst clicking cameras, I also informed him that he had not answered my question. He was puzzled by the response and quickly turned to pass out leaflets announcing "All Power to the Pie."

The newspapers found the incident irresistible. Only the *New York*

Times quoted my prediction that the press would play it up and overlook the two days of testimony. Because the pie thrower had signaled the press ahead of time, there were pictures for the front pages, to be adorned with headlines. I was variously identified as an "Obscenity Panelist," "Smut Prober," and "Pornography Fighter." The caption in the *Honolulu Star-Bulletin* read, "Cream Pie Was Cleanest Thing at This Hearing." The Akron *Beacon Journal* noted, "Yippie Witness Makes Custard Last Stand." Even the *New York Times* came through with "Pornography Commissioner Gets More Than an Eyeful of Cheesecake." Clearly, the hearing had become a form of theater.

Later came the editorials and a barrage of letters. A few applauded the turning of the cheek as a victory, but most favored an eye for an eye and a pie for a pie. Permissiveness was the most general complaint, and I was apparently regarded as the kind of professor who had created the wave of campus unrest.

The mail eventually subsided, but it picked up again after the report of the Commission was issued. This time, the charge of permissiveness thundered through the postal system, but not without some justification.

RECOMMENDATIONS: ADVICE AND DISSENT

By July 1969, one year after the creation of the Commission, unsolicited mail had become a problem for a great many other Americans. Congress had received numerous complaints about advertisements of sex material sent through the postal system, and the President had recommended legislation to protect householders against such mailings. All of this reached peak concern about the time that the Commission was to issue a progress report to Congress and to the President. It was also the time to seek further funding for the second year of Commission activity. For a brief time, the Commission acted in a politically sensitive manner.

A progress report was issued. It made no recommendations but noted that an extensive study was under way that would yield results on schedule. Not entirely by coincidence, and in order to give the policymakers a concrete illustration of Commission efforts, a tentative draft of a statute prepared by the legal panel for the control of unsolicited sexually explicit materials mailed to private residences was appended to the progress report. Some time later, Congress passed a law very similar to that

draft. It also approved an additional $1,100,000 as the Commission bud-
get for fiscal 1970. The first year, which included many panel meetings
and bimonthly sessions of the Commission, was thus extended for a complete term. And all of this happened even though Commissioner Hill
added a dissent to the progress report warning that the Commission was
going headlong into effects studies and that, if this continued, Congress
could not expect anything more in the final recommendations than proposals for laws on sales to minors, pandering, and the invasion of privacy.

One year later, seventeen Commissioners met for two long days in
a remote Virginia site to review panel reports, to reflect, and to recommend.

The first day was devoted to studying, questioning, and revising the
four panel reports, some of which still awaited final versions from some
of the field research. At that point, the panel reports were principally
summary drafts of research written by the staff. Later revisions by both
Commissioners and staff did not make fundamental alterations but were
directed to completing the presentations and adding polish to the form.
The effects panel, for example, spent one eighteen-hour day thereafter
checking details and phrasing.

The early draft of the effects report received the most thorough scrutiny and discussion of all panel reports on the first day of the meetings,
when recommendations were to be considered. Technical questions were
pursued with vigor. The sociologists were back in the classroom, answering
questions on the meaning of crime statistics, control groups, probability
sampling, correlation, interview-completion rates, and the like. Substantive
findings were also highlighted, and the consistent pattern of results challenging allegations of "harm" from exposure to erotica was reviewed in detail.

On the second day the focus shifted. Individual Commissioners expressed their own feelings and conclusions. Explicit reference to research
diminished. One sensed the appearance of outside reference groups. For
the sociologists, this did not greatly alter their stance because their reference group included other researchers. It was thus easier for them, in
their policy role, to move with the data. Others moved too, but more
selectively.

The major policy options turned around alternative statutes drafted
by the legal panel, and discussion centered on definitional distinctions

between textual and pictorial obscenity, the meaning of declaratory judgments, and the age that should be specified in juvenile obscenity laws. Selective reference to research was made now and then to reinforce a position being advanced.

Ultimately, the entire two-year experience boiled down to *ten recommendations* approved by a majority, with dissents appended by various minorities. Six of the recommendations directly involved legislation; four did not.

The central nonlegislative recommendation, the first listed in the Commission report, called for a massive sex education effort; ten characteristics of this program were described. Although this recommendation received strong approval from many sources, including commendation from the magazine of the National Parent-Teacher's Association,[22] most such responses were lost in the backwash of the initial negative official reaction to the report.

Also overlooked were most of the legislative proposals by the majority. Here Commissioner Hill's earlier forecast proved correct. The majority of the Commission recommended legislation restricting sale of pictorial material to juveniles and controlling the mailing and public display of explicit sex materials.

But the fallout from another recommendation, approved by twelve of seventeen participating members, precluded public recognition of any of the above. That bomb was marked as follows: *The Commission recommends that federal, state, and local legislation prohibiting the sale, exhibition, or distribution of sexual materials to consenting adults should be repealed.* Nine summary statements were attached in support of this recommendation, six of which drew directly from the empirical studies of the Commission.

CONCLUSION

Another full chapter would have to be written to analyze the response provoked by this one Commission proposal to repeal laws. That response, coming initially in an election year, was not all spontaneous. Nor was it

[22] "Light on the Darkness of Pornography," *The PTA Magazine*, November 1970, pp. 16–17.

all negative. In fact, one state, Hawaii, later adopted essentially all the majority legislative recommendations, including the one concerning the rights of consenting adults. The majority of the Commission believed that this would have been good national policy. The basis for it could have been set in the 1973 Supreme Court rulings, but it was not.

And yet we were not far from these proposals in matters of law and in matters of practice at the time the Commission recommendations were made. About five months before the Commission's report, in a unanimous decision in the *Stanley* case, the Supreme Court set a favorable climate for the Commission's recommendations. Speaking for the Court, Justice Marshall said, "If the First Amendment means anything, it means that a state has no business telling a man, sitting alone in his own house, what books he may read or what films he may watch." Continuing, he said, "Our whole constitutional heritage rebels at the thought of giving government the power to control men's minds." The First Amendment protects a man's "right to satisfy his intellectual and emotional needs in the privacy of his own home," even if he satisfied them by watching obscene movies, Justice Marshall said. Subsequently, a three-judge federal district court in Boston held that adults have a similar right to view whatever they wish in movie theaters: "If a rich Stanley can view a film in his home, a poorer Stanley should be free to visit a protected theater."

But courts make rulings, and directions change as justices come and go. Clearly, the current Court has not moved in the direction warranted by Commission data or by the implications of research. The new rulings decentralize decisions about obscenity law, but the old tests of "prurience" and "offensiveness" remain. "Redeeming social value" has been replaced by "serious literary, artistic, political, or scientific value" in the trio of standards. Much of what was within the Court's reach to clarify or resolve is now passed on to the local scene. Confusion on criteria and definitions will still be with us. The guidelines will not stimulate concern with effects studies as the Commission formulated them. Controls will be more varied. Innovation in restriction and repression of sex communication can be expected. Some new restrictions may only heighten rather than dampen curiosity. Obscenity laws have a way of becoming a kind of government "Bad Housekeeping Seal of Approval."

I believed that the Supreme Court has increased the probability of local mischief by ardent censors. However, it is conceivable that some states and localities will now, like Oregon and Hawaii, move in a direction consistent with the sum of the Commission's majority recommendations. But if they do, given the Court's guidelines, the argument will not be won by reference to sociological reasoning or social science data from the Commission, which could, in effect, and should, through a concern with effects studies, have altered the test for obscenity. That test continues on ambiguous grounds, where empirical proof or disproof of damaging personal or social harm are not relevant. Therein lies the Commission's failure, for the moment at least.

—————————————— CHAPTER TWO ——————————————

The Commission on Population Growth and the American Future
Its Origins, Operations, and Aftermath

—————————————— CHARLES F. WESTOFF ——————————————

Princeton University

THE BACKGROUND

The origins of the Commission on Population Growth and the American Future are most likely to be found in the pressures brought to bear on the White House and Congress from both the environmental concerns of the day, which had reached a shrill level in 1969 and 1970, and from the persistence of John D. Rockefeller 3rd, who had been pressing for such a development for some years. Such concerns had found a receptive ear in Daniel Patrick Moynihan, Counselor to the President, who had a special interest in the problems of urban growth and a belief in the importance of long-range planning.

The ecologist's concern for resource depletion and environmental deterioration had been picked up by youth on college campuses and had been publicized widely in the press. Paul Ehrlich, via his best-selling paperback, *The Population Bomb,* was becoming a folk hero to college students. Population growth had long been regarded as a serious problem for developing countries, but aside from the somewhat disrupting effects of the postwar baby boom, it had not caught the popular imagination as a domestic problem of any serious dimension. Now, however, despite the persistent decline in the birthrate, population growth in the United States was being cast in the role of a multiplier of the high levels of per capita consumption and the use of technology that disregards environmental stability, both of which were viewed as threatening the integrity of the ecosystem. Coupled with this new perspective of population growth was a moral concern that the United States, by virtue of its wealth, consumes a grossly disproportionate share of the world's resources, thus deprives other nations of their natural heritage. Therefore, population growth in the United States simply increased this "exploitation" of developing countries.

Rockefeller's interest in population had been cultivated for several decades. In 1952 he had founded the Population Council, which concentrated on problems of population growth in developing nations. He had just co-chaired (with Wilbur Cohen) the President's Committee on Population and Family Planning, appointed by President Johnson. Among this Committee's recommendations on family planning and population was the proposal to create a Commission to assess the consequences of population trends in the United States, to examine trends in world population growth, to evaluate progress in family planning, and to consider the consequences of alternative population policies.

The direct impetus to the birth of the Commission was the message to Congress by President Nixon delivered in July 1969. This was a comprehensive—some have called it eloquent, even inspirational—speech. The President called attention to the range of problems confronting the nation which could be traced, in part, to the rapid growth of population, and he called attention to the possibility of the addition of another 100 million Americans by the end of the century.

After emphasizing the seriousness of the growth of world population and the need for long-range planning, the President turned to the population question in the United States. The following excerpts give some of the flavor of the message:

> This growth will produce serious challenges to our society. I believe that many of our present social problems may be related to the

fact that we have had only fifty years in which to accommodate the second hundred million Americans. . . . And it now appears that we will have to provide for a third hundred million Americans in a period of just 30 years.

Where, for example, will the next hundred million Americans live? . . . Are our cities prepared for such an influx? The chaotic history of urban growth suggests that they are not and that many of their existing problems will be severely aggravated by a dramatic increase in numbers. Are there ways, then, of readying our cities? Alternatively, can the trend toward greater concentration of population be reversed?

What of our natural resources and the quality of our environment? . . . A growing population will increase the demand for such resources. . . . The ecological system upon which we now depend may seriously deteriorate if our efforts to conserve and enhance the environment do not match the growth of population.

How will we educate and employ such a large number of people? . . . How will we provide adequate health care. . . . Many of our institutions are already under tremendous strain as they try to respond to the demands of 1969. Will they be swamped by a growing flood of people in the next thirty years? Finally we must ask: how can we better assist American families so that they will have no more children than they wish to have? . . . Unwanted or untimely childbearing is one of several forces which are driving many families into poverty or keeping them in that condition . . . it needlessly adds to the burdens placed on all of our resources by increasing population.

Perhaps the most dangerous element in the present situation is the fact that so few people are examining these questions from the viewpoint of the whole society. . . . In the governmental sphere, however, there is virtually no machinery through which we can develop a detailed understanding of demographic changes and bring that understanding to bear on public policy.

It is for all these reasons that I today propose the creation by Congress of a Commission on Population Growth and the American Future.

One of the most serious challenges to human destiny in the last third of this century will be the growth of the population. Whether man's response to that challenge will be a cause for pride or for despair in the year 2000 will depend very much on what we do today. . . . When future generations evaluate the record of our time, one of the

most important factors in their judgment will be the way in which we
responded to population growth.

Some eight months after the President's message, the Congress en-
acted a statute in March 1970, creating the Commission on Population
Growth and the American Future for a period of two years. In his message, the President had emphasized the necessity of planning the accommodation of the next 100 million citizens. He wanted the Commission to
explore the course of population growth and internal migration to the year
2000, to assess the implications of such probable change on the public
sector of the national economy, and to evaluate its significance for the
activities of federal, state, and local government. It was in the House of
Representatives, under pressure from part of the population lobby, that
two additional and more controversial mandates were included: to assess
the implications of population growth for natural resources and for the
quality of the environment, and "the various means appropriate to the
ethical values and principles of this society by which our Nation can
achieve a population level properly suited for its environmental, natural
resources, and other needs." It was this last mandate that permitted the
Commission to interpret its basic charge as that of recommending a national population policy rather than developing a master plan to prepare
for continued population increase; the Commission preferred to regard
its mission as "interventionist" rather than "accommodationist." But unless one is prepared to believe that no one in the White House paid any
further attention, this outcome could hardly be viewed as a surprise
there, considering not only the President's appointment of Rockefeller as
the chairman, but also the number of people connected in one way or
another with the population movement who ultimately became members
of the Commission following White House clearance.

SELECTION OF THE COMMISSION

This Commission was thus a statutory creation by Congress; it was not
merely a presidential commission. This is an important distinction because it meant that the Commission was responsible to the legislative as
well as to the executive branch of the government, a consideration that
the Commission occasionally reminded itself of when possible White

House sensitivities were mentioned in connection with controversial topics.

The leaders of both parties in both the Senate and the House of Representatives nominated a total of four members of Congress who had shown some interest in population to serve on the Commission: Senator Joseph Tydings, a Democrat from Maryland who, after his defeat in the 1970 election, was replaced by Senator Alan Cranston of California, and Senator Robert Packwood, a young Republican from Oregon. The members of the House were Congressman John Blatnik, Democrat from Minnesota (replaced in the second year by James Scheuer of New York) and Congressman John Erlenborn, Republican from Illinois. With the exception of Erlenborn, who attended the meetings regularly, the participation of these Congressmen ranged from irregular to symbolic. Nevertheless, several kept in close touch through their legislative assistants and exerted some influence on the deliberations and the report of the Commission.

The remaining twenty members were selected in a process of nominations by the chairman and Moynihan, who originally served as liaison between the Commission and the White House. The aim of the chairman was to select a range of persons roughly representative of critical constituencies as well as persons knowledgeable about the broad subject matter and persons experienced in government. The White House, on the other hand, was presumably more concerned with political rather than with professional criteria. About half the nominees proposed to the White House were rejected.

The final list included a large proportion of distinguished citizens, such as the former head of the World Bank (George Woods); the then head of the Boise Cascade Company (Rober Hansberger); Mrs. Otis Chandler of the Los Angeles *Times* family; and quite a few distinguished social scientists (John Meyer of Yale and the National Bureau of Economic Research, Gale Johnson of the University of Chicago, and David Bell of the Ford Foundation), some of whom were drawn from the population field (Otis Dudley Duncan of the University of Michigan, Bernard Berelson of the Population Council, Margaret Bright of Johns Hopkins). There were members of the black community (including a physician, a college president, and a professor) a Mexican-American woman, a Puerto Rican, Catholics, physicians, and youth, one of whom was a nineteen-year-old student. Politically, the group was conservative by college student standards, liberal by national and White House standards. By no stretch of the imagination could the group be characterized as radical—a fact that influenced the outcome of several acrimonious debates about population policy and the political process.

ORGANIZATION OF THE STAFF

The process of forming the Commission consumed three months—one-eighth of its total lifetime. At this juncture, I was appointed as the Director of the Staff (on a two-thirds time basis) and began assembling a staff of some twenty persons, a task complicated by the fact that June is too late in the year to recruit academic people. Our Congressional appropriation was about $1.4 million ($.5 million less than the Pornography Commission, which may or may not be a revealing commentary on national priorities), and there was a ceiling on the number of staff that could be hired in different categories. Because of this limitation, as well as the time pressures, we were obliged to adopt a strategy of "contracting out" the bulk of the research. Even if such constraints had not prevailed, the large number and wide diversity of topics covered (about one hundred) meant that forming an adequate staff of highly qualified experts was simply impossible. Moreover, since we wanted the very best persons to address particular topics, the contract route was the only feasible one. (We deliberately established levels of honoraria that were attractive by academic standards in order to attract such people and to induce them to produce on fairly short time schedules).

The first staff appointment was the administrative assistant (without whose knowledge of bureaucratic routines, no Commission would even begin), and then a deputy director who was a professional demographer-sociologist (Robert Parke), whose activities were especially critical. The plan was to recruit research directors in the different substantive areas in which our research and deliberations were to be directed. Within a period of three to four months, most of the major appointments had been made—specialists in economics, political science and government, regional and urban planning, and public information. These experts added professional assistants and used consultants as the need arose. The primary responsibilities of the research directors were to formulate the specific research questions, to identify the appropriate scholars or organizations to undertake the research, to negotiate the arrangements, and ultimately to draft summaries of these and other materials for Commission meetings. In addition, we were all engaged in our own research focused on Commission questions. One such project was a national public opinion poll which we formulated to gauge public information about population and a wide range of attitudes toward population-related matters, such as city size, immigration, abortion, and population policy.

The enabling statute also permitted the Commission to draw upon the resources of other government agencies. We relied heavily on the Bureau of the Census and on several other agencies for population and economic projections, data on the characteristics of immigrants, and other subjects.

Most of the staff was also drawn from other government agencies. Aside from whatever advantages they may have perceived in ordinary job terms, the prospect of editing volumes of research papers was a special inducement, particularly for those imbued with academic values.

FORMULATION AND PROCEDURES

Much of the contracted research focused on the economic, environmental, political, and social consequences of population growth and distribution in the United States. This direction of research was questioned at the outset by several influential members of the Commission who expressed the view that the Commission ought not spend its time assessing the costs and benefits of population growth, but that it should concentrate on how to improve the quality of life by reducing the rate of growth (if not the size) of the population; and should spend the time designing ways of achieving this objective. This viewpoint was rejected by the majority, some of whom felt that the desirability of reducing population growth was a far from obvious objective. Thus, the evaluation of the consequences of growth rather than the means of reducing fertility became the paramount concern of the research effort.

Most of the members were not expert in demography and, since knowledge of the consequences of growth in developed societies was virtually nonexistent, there was an obvious need to provide some education in the first half of the Commission life. This took the form of circulating reading material, bringing in experts to lecture on different topics, and presentations by individual staff members. The members worked hard and contributed a significant portion of their time to homework and meetings. Later in the process, research that had been commissioned was made the topic of presentation. In the second half of the period the Commission was concerned with formulating the recommendations and with reviewing drafts of the report. The Commission always met as a whole (mostly in Washington); there were no task forces as such and, with minor exceptions, no subcommittees. The agenda for Commission meetings, which met monthly for two days and more frequently toward the end, were ordinarily initiated and organized by the Staff Director and approved by the Chairman.

In order to represent the views of organizations in some way connected with population (as distinct from the views of the public in general, presumably reflected in the opinion poll), as well as to publicize its work, the Commission elected to organize and hold five public hearings around the country. The hearings were loosely focused on particular topics—population distribution, ethnic concerns, abortion, and the environment. They began in Washington and the remaining hearings were held in widely scattered cities. Organizations such as churches, government agencies, different lobbies, health organizations, business associations, planning groups, and many others were invited to submit and present written testimony. The Commission was represented by a half-dozen or so members. These hearings typically lasted two days and were regarded as quite successful in terms of public relations and as good informational sources.

At midpoint, the Commission published an Interim Report, a short, highly publicized, and very well received statement of position and plans. Little in the way of conclusions had been reached because the Commission had been deliberating only for six months before it began reviewing drafts. The Interim Report described the demographic situation and the subjects it was exploring—the bases on which it intended to develop policy recommendations. It communicated important messages about the need to evaluate population growth and a perspective on the subject:

> We do not take future population trends as inevitable. . . . There is a need today for the Nation to consider population growth explicitly and to formulate policy for the future. . . . We regard population growth . . . as an intensifier or multiplier of many problems impairing the quality of life in the United States. . . . The best kind of national population policy would be one that serves the general welfare by promoting informed individual choice. . . .

This report was extremely successful: I cannot recall a single negative response from any quarter. It also undoubtedly contributed to enhancing the cohesiveness of the group.

ISSUES

Several important issues were developing, however, which frequently threatened to destroy this cohesiveness. One recurrent and pervasive disagreement involved the "narrow versus the broad" definition of the scope of the report. This had many manifestations and shifting alliances. The basic problem was the intrinsically diffuse nature of population effects. Given the view that population growth intensified social, environmental, governmental, and international problems at the macro level, and that unwanted childbearing created many problems at the individual family level, there were few "problems" that could not qualify as relevant. There was no logical solution to this question: the topics finally covered included most of the obvious ones and some peripheral ones that might be characterized as pet interests of a few members. Several topics that might have been covered were not—marriage and divorce, for example. The final coverage was thus, to some extent, arbitrary.

Another more crystallized disagreement, not unrelated to the question of scope, reflected different basic perceptions of the population problem itself. There was the ecological view, which held that population growth was just one, though an important, manifestation of man's insensitivity to his environment. This was frequently coupled with anti-big city, antitechnology, and antieconomic growth ideologies. As one of the statements of this view in the final report phrased it: "According to this view, nothing less than a different set of values toward nature, the transcendence of a laissez-faire market system, a redefinition of human identity in terms other than consumerism, and a radical change if not abandonment of the growth ethic, will suffice." Perhaps no more than five of the twenty-four members coalesced around this ecological perspective, but their position was greatly strengthened by the force of several of the personalities involved.

Most frequently in opposition to the ecological perspective was what might be called the "unwanted fertility" school. In this view, the population growth problem was seen as the consequence of the lack of control of fertility, which was to be solved by promoting equal access to the means of control and enhancing couples' opportunities to exercise freedom of choice. The population problem was regarded "more as the sum of such individual problems than as a societal problem transcending the interests of individuals," although the reduction of unwanted fertility was seen as making a significant contribution to the stabilization of population growth. This is a much less radical view than the ecological one. It calls for education, information, and government subsidy rather than for new values or fundamental changes in the economy and government.

The third perspective—the social justice view—was different but not independent of the elements in the first two views. Population was not high on the agenda of priorities of the ethnic minority members. The deprivation of economic opportunity and the injustice of the prevailing distribution of income was the main concern; unwanted fertility was a symptom of unequal opportunity, but population policy was no substitute for the redistribution of income. This group (four or five members with sympathetic support from all) sided with those who wanted to broaden the concept of population policy; ideologically, it found the antiestablishment views of the ecological minority at least superficially compatible.

These three perspectives lie beneath many of the discussions and most of the differences that prevailed within the Commission, differences that were in part reflected within the staff as well. The negotiated solution was to express the difference as "A Diversity of Views" in the Introduction to the Final Report. The irony of the situation was that the sharply delineated and frequently acrimonious debates had significance primarily for the diagnosis of the population problem; they had few consequences for the final policy recommendations. They were symbolic positions on which people felt they had to take an ideological stand—positions that certainly affected and perhaps even inflamed the rhetoric—but that had little bearing on the recommendations that were made. As stated in the Introduction, "Despite the different perspectives from which population is viewed, all of the population policies we shall recommend are consistent with all three positions." Thus, there was much more blood shed over the diagnosis than over the prescription. This was not because the logic of the positions did not lead to different policy conclusions, but rather because everyone more-or-less recognized that any impact the Commission report might have would be seriously affected by the political and moral acceptability of the recommendations.

By no means were these the only differences that appeared during the twenty-one months of meetings, but they did overshadow and pervade many other disagreements. Differences of opinion emerged predictably in the debate over abortion, but they were highly structured and were resolved by the filing of dissenting statements at the end of the report. More excitement and a more complicated pattern of disagreement developed over the immigration question, which yielded several competing views: the liberal view that, for historical, cultural, and foreign policy reasons, the volume of immigration should not be reduced; the view that immigration, which was currently contributing 20 percent of annual population growth, should be somewhat curtailed; the ethnic arguments that immigrants competed for jobs with members of minority groups (someone reported that there were more Filipino than black doctors in the United States, and therefore that immigration should be reduced); and the view that illegal aliens competing for jobs were the real problem, especially in the Southwest. A compromised set of recommendations on immigration was the outcome.

Despite all of these differences in opinion, the Commission was aware of the political importance of achieving consensus (consensus is to some extent a function of deadlines), and there was a considerable amount of compromise from all quarters. Nevertheless, some minority statements were filed and published in the final report. These focused primarily on abortion (four members dissented from the majority position, each with a different individual position), but ranged over other miscellaneous topics as well: some were simply amplifications of supporting views. With the exception of the separate statements on abortion, it is reasonable to conclude that there was a high degree of consensus in the report of this Commission.

SOCIAL RESEARCH AND POLICY FORMATION

What significance for the final report and for its recommendations did the enormous amount of social science research commissioned actually have? Apart from its scientific and educational value, did the research activity of the Commission have any pronounced impact on the substance of the report? Perhaps the most useful way of formulating the question is to ask whether and in what ways the final report would have differed if the research had not been done.

The answer, predictably, is more complicated than the question, but on balance, I believe that the research did make a real difference. It probably had little if any effect on the philosophic spirit of the report: the same competing frames of reference would have been advanced and probably resolved in the same way because they were essentially different views of the world, largely outside of the jurisdiction of scientific adjudication. Much of the rhetoric, some of it pious and euphemistic (euphemism is the language of public policy) would have been the same. And many of the recommendations that grew out of deeply rooted convictions, such as the abortion recommendation, would not have changed. But the research, much of which was addressed to policy issues, did penetrate and influence some of the basic conclusions about the effects of population growth and about policy recommendations.

The largest contract and one of the most important research conclusions came from a study of the role of population growth in the depletion of resources and in environmental deterioration. The overall conclusion was that population growth played a minor role in the short run (thirty to fifty years) as compared with technological, economic, and government policy considerations. In the longer run, population growth would become increasingly important. The message for population policy, therefore, was that resource and environmental considerations implied prudence rather than crisis; that there were no benefits to be realized from continued growth, but that population was an indirect and ineffectual policy lever for environmental problems. This general conclusion dominated the tone of the chapter on this subject in the final report. It made a critical contribution to the debates on this subject within the Commission.

The demographic work involved in the use of population projections was critical to the analysis of the consequences of growth. The general methodology employed was to compare the consequences (economic, environmental, public sector expenditures) of the two- versus the three-child family (both population size and associated age distributions). Basic demographic analysis also underlaid the descriptions of alternative paths (varying the average number of births, the maternal age, and the timing of childbearing), which figured prominently in the Commission's description of the road to population stabilization.

Several other demographic calculations contributed importantly to the Commission's deliberations and recommendations. In one instance, it was demonstrated that if women averaged 2.0 rather than 2.1 births, zero population growth could be achieved near the same level and in almost the same time with immigration continued at the current volume. Although not a world-shaking scientific discovery, this bit of demographic intelligence was extremely important in the debate over immigration policy and was influential in defeating a recommendation to reduce the volume.

Another demographic exercise that influenced policy was directed toward evaluating the demographic capability of national "growth center strategy" (a policy being evaluated within the government to use government spending to divert population away from the large metropolitan areas to smaller, viable cities). It could be shown that even under the most optimistic assumptions about the success of such a policy, it could make only a small dent in the expected growth of metropolitan areas over the next thirty years because of the overwhelming impact of natural increase in the metropolitan areas. Thus, whatever other merits such a policy might have, it would be foolish indeed to expect that it would significantly influence the size of metropolitan populations.

One of the most important applications of social science research to policy formation came out of the National Fertility Studies of 1965 and 1970. It makes an absolutely critical difference in the nature of population policy whether the stabilization of population can be achieved largely through the prevention of unwanted fertility or whether more radical social changes are necessary to alter the number of children desired. The estimates of the incidence of unwanted births derived from these two surveys revealed that the elimination of unwanted fertility would take the nation most of the way to replacement (and considering current fertility levels, well below replacement). One cannot overestimate the policy significance of this finding. Instead of trying to change a social norm through politically difficult means, the Commission could concentrate instead on trying to provide the means to satisfy couples' apparent goals through the improvement and distribution of methods of fertility control, a "solution" well within acceptable political limits. Such a solution had everything. It implied helping people to achieve what they want; it did not imply any radical solutions to the problem of population growth. Aside from abortion, it was singularly unobjectionable; it was theoretically easy to do; and its costs were low! It was difficult to imagine a policy with more political promise.

The study of unwanted fertility yielded other policy-relevant find-

ings. The negative relationship between income and unwanted births provided a further rationale for government subsidization of family planning
for the poor. And the corroboration of the hypothesis that race differences
in rates of population growth were almost entirely a function of differences in rates of unwanted fertility, greatly cooled this frequently heated
debate about an ideologically sensitive issue.

Many other studies also contributed to the report. Analysis of the
implications for the costs of education and health resulting from the age
distributions and growth associated with the two- versus the three-child
fertility rates contributed materially to the evidence in favor of a slower
growth rate and an older population. At the microeconomic level, a study
by economists of the considerable direct and indirect costs of rearing and
educating a child was widely publicized, which undoubtedly had some
effect on people's thinking on the subject.

The discovery of the appalling amount of ignorance about population
in the general public (e.g., 60 percent did not know and could not guess
the size of the United States population within ± 50 million) provided a
basis for recommendations about population education. A survey finding
that only 20 percent of sexually active, unmarried teen-age girls report
using any contraception regularly, dramatized the recommendation of the
provision of such information and services to minors. The public opinion
poll supplemented this by revealing that nearly two-thirds of the public
approved of high schools offering information to teen-agers on ways of
avoiding pregnancy, a statistic that was of some value in the subject of
sex education.

The public opinion poll also indicated that half of the public felt that
abortion ought to be a matter decided solely between individuals and
their physicians, a statistic that was used to support the liberal abortion
recommendation.

The Commission also tapped into another study done in New York
City, which indicated that population density per se was virtually irrelevant to juvenile delinquency and mental illness. This "negative" finding
was useful in evaluating some of the laboratory research with animals that
had indicated increases in aggressive and antisocial behavior when population density reached certain levels.

These, then, are illustrations of some (but not all) of the applications
of social science research to the formation of policy by the Population
Commission. This research was of great importance to the nature of the

diagnosis as well as to the prescription. Some of it was critical to the direction of the argument and the policies; others were useful in supporting preconceived judgments.

Would the final report have differed if social science dominated the Commission even more than it did (which was considerable)? In my opinion, probably not. (Fewer pieties but perhaps more obfuscation.) Yet, different individual social scientists with different ideological views might easily have altered the picture. One could readily conceive of much more radical population policy proposals that would concentrate on income redistribution or on more basic changes designed to alter the value of children in the society.

AFTERMATH

The Commission elected to publish the final report in three sections over a period of several weeks. This decision was reached in order to extend the publicity that it would receive; particularly, to avoid having the abortion issue dominate the publicity. The first section covered the diagnosis of the population question; the second section detailed the recommendations, primarily those connected with reproduction; the third section included recommendations on immigration, population distribution, and the organization of population statistics and research in the government.

The strategy was fairly successful in maintaining the report in public view over a longer period of time than it might have otherwise received. But the second section, containing the abortion recommendation, was treated by the media exactly as the Commission had anticipated—with abortion headlines.

Editorial comment on the report as a whole was highly favorable across the nation. It was uniformly praised with adjectives like "sane," "balanced," "intelligent," "sensitive," "thoughtful," "frank," and so on. The first negative response came from the Catholic Church in the form of a statement released by the National Catholic Bishops' Conference, which unanimously denounced the report primarily for its stand on abortion but also, more generally, for what they regarded as the Commission's materialistic view of the "quality of life." Protestant and Jewish groups, on the other hand, were enthusiastic about the report and were applying pressure on the White House for response.

Two months had now elapsed without any reaction from the President. (Although various individual Congressmen had reacted favorably, there never was any formal Congressional response as such.) President Nixon's response, issued in May 1972, was a disappointment at every level. After some acclaim for the importance of the research for government planning, the President reiterated his personal opposition to abortion and disagreed with the recommendation that contraceptive information and services be made available to minors, on the grounds that this would weaken the family. No attention at all was directed to the basic analysis of the costs and benefits of population growth and the conclusion that population stabilization was desirable. In effect, the response was narrowly political and greatly at variance with the concerns about population that the President had expressed less than three years earlier. The environmental fever had diminished, the birthrate had fallen, and the Census Bureau had revised downward its projection of population growth. And it was an election year.

If the President's response were the only criterion of the Commission's efforts, then it would have to be judged a failure. But that is not the case. The report has featured prominently in the activities of at least one congressional committee and has been used in various ways in government departments responsible for family planning, population research and statistics, population education, and other topics within the subject of population distribution. Perhaps of even greater long-run importance than immediate action by the executive or legislative branches is the educational and the international impact that the report is having and will continue to have.

Early in the Commission deliberations, a plan was adopted to produce a video as well as a written report. Originally, the plan was to purchase an hour of prime time on one of the commercial television networks with privately raised funds. Although the three major networks were initially enthusiastic, they ultimately declined to sell the time when the Commission insisted on complete editorial autonomy. (A complaint was subsequently brought before the Federal Communications Commission charging the networks with being unresponsive to their public service responsibilities.) A film was made by an independent producer and was shown on national public television last fall. The reception by the press was favorable. However, the White House subsequently exerted pressure on HEW to prevent it from circulating the film to high schools, colleges, and other groups around the country. Private funds were used to accomplish the goal.

Aside from its contribution to the education of the public on population matters, the Commission, through its research reports, will be making important additions to scholarly knowledge, particularly on the consequences of population growth.

The Population Commission represented an important effort by an advanced country to develop a national population policy—the basic thrust of which was to slow growth in order to maximize the "quality of life." It is quite likely that even though this effort has not been officially adopted as national policy, it is being regarded as an important step, if not a model for other countries. For example, the recently released report of a similar panel in Great Britain has drawn on the United States report; there have also been important contacts with comparable groups in Australia and the Netherlands.

The year 1974 was World Population Year. In preparation the United Nations organized various committees and symposia. One of these— charged with developing the World Population Plan of Action for submission to delegates from member governments at the 1974 conference—was also influenced by this report. As a Latin American member of the Committee commented: "Your report may have more influence in the rest of the world than it will in your own country."

The National Commission on the Causes and Prevention of Violence
Reflections on the Contributions of Sociology and Sociologists

———————————— JAMES F. SHORT, JR. ————————————

Washington State University and Stanford University

Politically, the National Commission on the Causes and Prevention of Violence was a "crisis" commission, appointed by President Lyndon Johnson in the dark hours following the assassination of Senator Robert F. Kennedy—or, more properly, presidential candidate Robert F. Kennedy, because the presidency has been the most vulnerable of all political offices in this country to assassination. However, the problems with which the Violence Commission was concerned were, and are, of long standing. As we observed in the Commission's *Progress Report*,

> . . . Violence is but one facet of man living with his fellow men. Throughout history men have sought to control violence, to institutionalize it and to regulate the form it takes, to make some forms of violence serve their collective needs and desires and to place other forms of violence beyond the pale. Violence becomes sharply separated into the basic categories of "legitimate" and "illegitimate" primarily in the context of particular human society or cultural tradition.

The knowledge that another commission had been appointed did little to assuage my fears and concerns over the violence and despair that seemed so pervasive in the country at that time. Furthermore, I had only recently resigned from the Graduate Deanship of my university and I was looking forward to the opportunity to complete long delayed research and writing projects. Those prospects seemed more realistic and important to me than did work of another national commission devoted to the violence of our time.

Yet, despite initial and persistent misgivings about the enterprise, I committed a sizable portion of my time and energies to the Violence Commission.

Sociologists and other social scientists did make important contributions to the work of the Commission, but a variety of circumstances combined to diminish the influence of these contributions on the Commission's *Final Report*. Chief among those circumstances were: (1) the extremely limited time frame of the Commission; (2) the composition of the Commission and its staff; and (3) the informal communications and normative system that characterized its operation; and (4) the lack of adequate scientific knowledge with clear policy implications. Our failure to be more effective was due also to organizational problems characteristic of sociology as a discipline and, by and large, of the entire academic community.

Because I think the organizational matters are crucial and not generally understood, I will first address points (2) and (3) by comparing the participation of lawyers and social scientists in the activities of the Commission.

LAWYERS, SOCIAL SCIENTISTS, AND THE NATIONAL INTEREST

Lawyers probably serve on and with more commissions than any other group, generally commissions appointed "in response to crises" more frequently than "technical" commissions. Some may argue that this is precisely the problem, but that is not my purpose. Ours is designed to be a government of laws, and to the extent that the types of crises that occasion the appointment of national commissions influence, and are influenced by, government, the law must surely be involved. But this is an insufficient explanation for the preponderance of lawyers on many com missions, because these matters are of great interest to the entire society, and their explanation and remedy often lie outside the law. The explanation lies rather in the nature of our political organization, in interest group politics, and in the organization of the legal profession.

At its more affluent and powerful levels, the legal profession is organized to respond quickly and effectively to the so-called national interest.[1] Lawyers, more clearly than sociologists, apparently perceive that the national interest represents their own interests, individually and collectively. Political and economic advantages do flow to lawyers who serve on governmental bodies. But sociologists perceive that such service is seen by the profession as at best peripheral, at worst, as evidence of having "sold out."[2]

The movement of lawyers— to and from large firms throughout the country, in and out of Washington, for service at all levels of government —is a well known phenomenon. I can illustrate this phenomenon in the context of the "balance" of the Violence Commission and its staff.

Popper refers to Lowe's notion of "interest group liberalism," by which "representatives of major sectors of American society participate, collectively in arriving at consensus on policy," as the "iron law of presidential appointment."[3] The Violence Commission exemplifies the type: its chairman, Milton S. Eisenhower, from "the other political party" vis-a-vis the President, had many distinguished qualifications, including an impeccable name. He was a former Special Ambassador and Presidential Representative for Latin American Affairs, and he had been president of three universities. He was the hardest working of the Commissioners, who undoubtedly read every word of every document published by the Commission, in draft as well as in final version. And he wrote extensive passages of the Commission Report. He was also a fair but expeditious chairman, fully supportive of the scholarly efforts of the staff, and in-

[1]The phrase, "the national interest," has no clear or specific meaning. Although it may be used to corrupt thought (Orwell, 1954), that is not my intent. In the immediate context I refer both to the interests of disciplines and professions (an identity which lawyers have realized more fully and successfully than have sociologists), and to the larger societal interests (or opposed to narrowly nationalistic or even political interests) to which in a larger sense we must be responsive.

[2]Richard Quinney. "Review Symposium." American Sociological Review, Vol. 36, No. 4, August 1971, pp. 724–727.

[3]Frank Popper. The President's Commission (New York: Twentieth Century Fund, 1970).

fluenced on a number of issues by those efforts. The Commission was politically balanced in other ways: major parties, liberal–conservative, houses of Congress, and even regional Congressional representation (Democrats Senator Philip A. Hart of Michigan and Representative Hale Boggs of Louisiana, Republican Senators Roman L. Hruska of Nebraska and William McCulloch of Ohio). Other Commissioners were similarly distinguished. They included a representative of the church (Terence Cardinal Cooke of New York); two jurists (A. Leon Higginbotham, U. S. District Court, Eastern District of Pennsylvania and Ernest W. McFarland, Arizona Supreme Court, a former Governor and U. S. Senator from that state); a female (former Dean of the Law School at Howard University and former Ambassador to Luxembourg, Patricia Roberts Harris); two other lawyers (Leon Jaworski, former Special Assistant U. S. Attorney General associated with federal enforcement of school integration policies and Army Chief of War Trials in World War II, and Albert E. Jenner, Jr., President of the National Conference Commission on Uniform State Laws, a conservative Republican who headed the legal team challenging the constitutionality of the House Un-American Activities Committee); a longshoreman, author, philosopher, and Presidential favorite, Eric Hoffer; and psychiatrist W. Walter Menninger, member of the National Advisory Health Council and Consultant to the Federal Bureau of Prisons and the Peace Corps.[4]

Balance was intended, if not achieved, in another respect. Both Judge Higginbotham, elected by his fellow commissioners as Vice-Chairman, and Ambassador Harris are black. But Popper notes that "extremists" are "not represented at all" on national commissions. Commissioners Higginbotham and Harris were acutely aware of their status in this

[4]The Violence Commission exemplifies another characteristic attributed to national commissions by Popper, "that the same names appear again and again," Judge Higginbotham had been a member of the President's Committee to Fulfill These Rights (White House Conference on Civil Rights) and of the Commission on Reform of the U.S. Criminal Law; Congressman Boggs was a member of the Warren Commission (to investigate the assassination of President John F. Kennedy); Cardinal Cooke was a member of the Presidential Task Force on International Developments; Mr. Jaworski was a member of the Crime Commission (The President's Commission on Law Enforcement and Administration of Justice); Mr. Jenner had served as Senior Counsel to the Warren Commission; and Congressman McCulloch had been a member of the Kerner Commission (The National Advisory Commission on Civil Disorders). They and the remaining members of the Commission had achieved national prominence in other respects as well.

respect. Early one morning, in the banter that customarily preceded Commission deliberations, one of the Commissioners noted cheerfully that "At least no one can say blacks aren't well represented on this Commission." Judge Higginbotham responded quickly with a chuckle, "Oh no. You've got it all wrong. The word is, Higginbotham's Negro, Harris she's colored, and we blacks aren't represented at all." There was much good humor about the matter, but everyone recognized its seriousness.

Three of the members of the Commission listed their profession as attorney at law, two were sitting judges, and four were members of Congress, all with legal training. The prominence of lawyers at the staff level was equally impressive. Executive Director Lloyd N. Cutler, like the Commissioners appointed by the President, is a senior partner in a Washington, D.C. law firm. He has a long record of distinguished governmental service. The deputy that he had chosen, Thomas D. Barr, was a partner in a similarly prestigious Wall Street firm. General Counsel James S. Campbell was a Justice Department employee and a former clerk for Supreme Court Justice William O. Douglas. The senior staff was rounded out by Air Force Colonel William G. McDonald, recruited from the Defense Department; Joseph Laitin, Director of Information, a longtime newspaper man who had served the White House in a similar capacity; and Co-Directors of Research, Short and Wolfgang.

Colonel McDonald, James Campbell, and Robert Baker (another young Justice Department lawyer) were the first recruits to the Commission staff. Fifteen out of twenty-five Task Force Directors in the history of the Commission were lawyers, including another Supreme Court clerk (for Justice Hugo Black). Other lawyers served on their staffs and as special assistants to the Commissioners. Most of these were recruited specifically for Commission tasks, although a few, notably the Congressional aides, were performing in their "normal" capacities. They came from influential law firms throughout the country and from a variety of governmental agencies. Most were young, bright, confident; and they know their way around Washington. Their recruitment was a relatively simply matter of contact by telephone between the director (or his delegate) and personal acquaintances in the firms and agencies whence they came. Like the Commissioners, however, the staff lawyers tended not to represent in their experience those aspects of the law that infringe most directly on the issues and groups most closely related to violence. There were no poverty lawyers, for example, or criminal lawyers. One Task Force co-director was a civil rights lawyer, and consultants rounded out the picture somewhat.

ENTER THE ACADEMIC COMMUNITY

When I contacted Commission Chairman Milton Eisenhower for informa-tion, he said that at its first meeting, the Commission unanimously agreed that extensive research was necessary as a basis for analysis and recom-mendations concerning the causes and prevention of violence; that more was needed than compromise of our preconceptions. For this purpose, the Commission looked to the academic community.

The first social science input to the Commission occurred when Cut-ler and Campbell traveled around the country shortly after their appoint-ments, consulting at both universities and foundations. According to Campbell their effort was twofold, (1) to seek advice as to how the Com-mission should proceed; and (2) to counteract the disillusionment of the academic community with the administration's handling of the Kerner Commission report, the war, and the atmosphere of violence that was so pervasive at that time. They sought to make the role of scholars promi-nent in this Commission

And they were successful. Out of these initial decisions and consulta-tions came the idea of an academic advisory panel and a conference of scholars to aid the Commission. Marvin Wolfgang also became associated with the Commission as a result of these consultations. He had been con-tacted by General Counsel James Campbell on behalf of the Executive Director, to come to Washington shortly after appointment of the Com-mission. His task: to help organize and to chair a conference of social and behavioral scientists for the purpose of advising the Commission as to its goals and procedures. The idea of the conference came from Cutler and Campbell, but it was enthusiastically endorsed by Eisenhower and ap-proved by the full Commission. The Conference was held on July 9 and 10, a month following the event that occasioned the appointment of the Commission. On short notice, forty-seven biologists, criminologists, his-torians, political scientists, psychiatrists, psychologists, sociologists, and lawyers—most from academic settings, but a few from government agencies and private clinics and corporations—attended. The discussions were lively, and memoranda setting forth their ideas were prepared by several participants. An academic advisory panel of ten members (five of whom had attended the Conference) was appointed shortly thereafter. Early in the life of the Commission the panel served as consultants and, throughout, as reactors to staff-prepared documents and in other ways.

Cutler and Campbell hoped that Wolfgang could be persuaded to assume the post of Director of Research for the Commission. He declined the invitation because he was committed to spend the following academic year at Cambridge (at the Institute of Criminology and Churchill College). But he agreed to serve in this capacity until a replacement could be found. On July 24 I was asked to become Director of Research and, by mutual agreement, Wolfgang and I became Co-Directors. The collaboration was close much of the time, although, of necessity, I had to deal with the day-to-day problems. We had a direct telephone line from the Commission offices to Wolfgang's Cambridge apartment, and he returned frequently for Commission business.

By the time that Wolfgang was summoned to meet with Cutler and Campbell, the plans to organize a staff of competent young lawyers to carry out staff work on the Commission were well under way. Wolfgang demurred, pointing out that the Commission's charge called primarily for expertise in the academic disciplines concerned with human behavior and institutions, rather than in the law per se. Cutler and Campbell agreed, and they were anxious to enlist the active participation of scholars. However, they were skeptical—in fact, distrustful—of the ability of social scientists to administer the staff work, to function effectively in the federal bureaucracy, and to get the job done in the short time span allowed. But a compromise was reached: Task Forces would be co-directed by a lawyer and a social scientist.

MANDATE AND ORGANIZATION

The presidential mandate to the Violence Commission was broad, and—for a social scientist, compelling, "I ask you," it said, "to undertake a penetrating search for the causes and prevention of violence—a search into our national life, our past as well as our present, our traditions as well as our institutions, our culture, our customs and our laws." This mandate was accompanied by more specific "Functions of the Commission," indicated in the Executive Order establishing the Commission:

> The Commission shall investigate and make recommendations with respect to:
>
> a   The causes and prevention of lawless acts of violence in our society including assassination, murder, and assault;
> b   The causes and prevention of disrespect for law and order, of disrespect for public officials, and of violent disruptions of public order by individuals and groups, and
> c   Such other matters as the President may place before the Commission.

Despite the Presidential focus on "lawless acts of violence," the Commission initially adopted a neutral definition of violence; that is, "the threat or use of force that results, or is intended to result, in the injury or forcible restraint or intimidation of persons, or the destruction or forcible seizure of property." The lack of implicit value judgment in this definition was a guiding principle of the staff research effort, and we were able to get Commission agreement in this initial Commission report on some of the implications of such a definition.

> There is no implicit value judgment in this definition. The maintenance of law and order falls within it, for a policeman may find it necessary in the course of duty to threaten or use force, even to injure or kill an individual. Wars are included within this definition, as is some punishment of children. It also includes police brutality, the violence of the Nazis, and the physical abuse of a child.
>
> This definition . . . helps us to recognize that illegitimate violence, like most deviant behavior, is on a continuum with and dynamically similar to legitimate violence. . . . A neutral definition of violence also helps us to recognize that some minimum level of illegitimate violence is to be expected in a free and rapidly changing industrial society. Maintaining a system of law enforcement capable of eliminating all illegitimate individual and group violence might so increase the level of legitimate violence that the harm to other values would be intolerable. A totalitarian police state, however efficient its use of violence might be in preserving order, would destroy the freedom of all. . . .

Man's effort to control violence has been one part, a major part, of his learning to live in society. The phenomenon of violence cannot be understood or evaluated except in the context of that larger effort.[5]

The Commission retreated from this neutral definition in its final report, concentrating its attention on "all illegal violence, including group violence, as incompatible with the survival of a just, democratic, and humane society," and insisting "emphatically" that "aggrieved groups must be permitted to exercise their constitutional rights of protest and public presentation of grievances." The contemporary political significance of collective violence was thereby blunted, although the role of violence in American political and social history continued to receive emphasis.[6] This difference in emphasis was the primary difference between the prevailing perspectives of the Commission and those advanced in several of the staff reports.

The Commission adopted a plan of task force staff organization focused on seven topics, which effectively structured the work of the staff. The seven task forces, their directors, and reports are listed as follows.

The task force organization by topic.

Task Force	(Co) Director	Report
Historical and Comparative Studies	Hugh Davis Graham Ted Robert Gurr	*Violence in America* (Vols. 1 and 2)
Demonstrations, Protests, and Group Violence	Jerome Skolnick	*The Politics of Protest: Violence Aspects of Protest and Confrontation* (Vol. 3).
Individual Acts of Violence	Donald J. Mulvihill Melvin Tumin Lynn A. Curtis (Assistant Director)	*Crimes of Violence* (Vols. 11, 12, and 13)
Assassination	James F. Kirkham Sheldon G. Levy William J. Crotty	*Assassination and Political Violence* (Vol. 8)

[5] *Progress Report*, p. 3.
[6] *Final Report*, p. 59.

Task Force	(Co) Director	Report
Firearms	George D. Newton, Jr. Franklin E. Zimring (Dir. of Research)	*Firearms and Violence* *in American Life* *(Vol. 7)*
The Media	Robert K. Baker Sandra J. Ball David L. Lange (General Counsel)	*Mass Media and* *Violence (Vol. 9):* *Hearings on Mass* *Media and Violence* *(Vol. 9A)*
Law and Law Enforcement	James S. Campbell Joseph R. Sahid David P. Stang*	*Law and Order Re-* *considered (Vol. 10)*

*During the first part of the Commission's existence this Task Force was directed by George L. Saunders, Jr. and LeRoy D. Clark.

Thus, attention was directed to historical and comparative perspectives, group and individual acts of violence (as descriptive rather than analytical categories), a particular act of violence (assassination), two assumed major influences (firearms and mass media), and control through law. The substantive categories are distinguished more by their public and political appeal than by their etiological significance—a not surprising consequence of the concern of the Commission with "what to do about" the problems they were studying. With certain notable exceptions, the Commissioners were more persons of "action" than of "thought," and they felt pressure to "recommend" to the President and to the American public. One can sympathize with Judge Higginbotham's expressed "personal sense" of "commission frustration" and his call for "a national moratorium on . . . commissions to probe the causes of racism, or poverty, or crime, or the urban crisis," while recognizing that those causes still are not well understood, and while questioning the advisability—in view of the lack of greater knowledge of both causes and clear policy guidelines—of "the prompt implementation" of the recommendations of past commissions.[7]

Even the categories chosen for study were the result as much of informal discussion by the young lawyers first recruited by the Director as of Commission deliberation, although the Commission made the final deci-

[7] *Final Report*, 1969, pp. 116–117.

sion. I am told "on reliable authority" that a Task Force on war was also suggested, but that the idea was abandoned because of the potentially explosive nature of such a direct focus on war in general and on the conflict in Indochina in particular. Instead, war was to be included in the province of the Task Forces on History and Comparative Perspectives, and on Demonstrations, Protests, and Group Violence. The effect of this decision was to focus attention on the war in Indochina as a source of social disruption, rather than on the political responsibilities for warmaking and its consequences, as sources of great division within our society and in other parts of the world. The Task Force on Group Violence (Demonstrations, Protests, and Group Violence) vigorously promoted the latter perspective in its report, *The Politics of Protest*. For a variety of reasons, that report was unacceptable to the Commission, and assessment of responsibilities for the war as a source of disruption was not systematically addressed by the Commission.

TASK FORCE OPERATION

Operation of the Task Forces was guided by the lawyer–social scientist collaborations originally agreed upon, but the compromise did not always work well and had many problems. A few contacts with social scientists had been made before I began working with the Commission, but senior colleagues were especially difficult to recruit and slow to come aboard; most had other commitments that interfered with full-time Commission service, and few could spend much time in the Commission offices. I could not devote full time to Commission activities until after the American Sociological Association and Society for the Study of Social Problems meetings at the end of August; nor could any other social scientist.

The young lawyers were there, however, and their senior counterparts were close at hand to advise and to constrain. They were accustomed to the pressure-cooker atmosphere of crash preparations, and they were more familiar with government operations and with Washington bureaucracies. They were accustomed to the quick gathering and assimilation of concrete facts and their use in advocacy, in contrast to the more deliberative academic style of research and preference for abstract theoretical formulations in the search for knowledge.

The lawyer's approach to problems was generally preferred by the Commissioners, who felt compelled to mashal facts quickly in order to reach plausible, if not entirely acceptable, conclusions and make recommendations to the President and to the public. They, after all, far more than the staff, were "on the line" with respect to reputation and constituencies represented. Conflicts were inevitable. In addition, the formal specifications of equal decision-making power between lawyers and social scientists were undermined by the informal norms, values, and communication networks that existed among the staff lawyers and between the lawyers and some of the Commissioners. Additionally, most academicians are not prepared to function effectively in the Washington bureaucracy where these same norms, values, and communication networks prevail. These structural constraints and the incredible pressures of time, combined with the lack of reliable and immediately available knowledge were, I suspect, the most crucial sources of disharmony between social scientists and lawyers, and the fundamental bases for our lack of greater effectiveness.

Yet it would be a mistake to overemphasize cases of personal disharmony between lawyers and social scientists. There were many instances of intense and harmonious collaboration, and disharmony was not limited to lawyers and social scientists. Indeed, a few instances of conflict between social scientists were as bitter as any between lawyers and social scientists. The importance of interpersonal conflict was overshadowed by the balance of influence on the Commission's activities which these factors combined to produce. Especially important, as noted above, were the crucial early discussions concerning the operation and the focus of the Commission. The choice of a director, his choice of personnel, and their ready availability greatly influenced task specification as well as task performance in the division of labor of the Commission.

In the end, only three task forces had lawyer and social scientist co-directors: those studying Crimes of Violence (sociologist Melvin Tumin, who could devote only part-time service to the Commission, and lawyer Donald Mulvihill, with special assistance from sociologist graduate student Lynn A. Curtis); Assassination and Political Violence (social psychologist Sheldon G. Levy and political scientist William J. Crotty, and lawyer James F. Kirkham); and Mass Media and Violence (sociologist Sandra J. Ball and lawyer Robert K. Baker, with David L. Lange as General Counsel). We tried to recruit a social scientist to co-direct the Task Force on

Law and Law Enforcement. Jerome Skolnick was first contacted for this purpose, but he chose instead to direct the Task Force on Violent Aspects of Protest and Confrontation. Two other social scientists were contacted and spent some time conferring with the staff. One of them agreed to serve as a consultant, but neither would be Co-Director of the Task Force. It was deemed unnecessary that a lawyer co-direct the Task Force on Historical and Comparative Perspectives, and historian Hugh Davis Graham and political scientist Ted Robert Gurr directed a very successful effort. University of Chicago Law School lawyer Franklin E. Zimring had previously studied the role of firearms in crime, and he was engaged to enlarge that effort for the Commission. He was joined parttime by fellow Chicago lawyer George D. Newton, Jr.

The Task Force on Group Violence was unique in that it was located physically in Berkeley, California, and also because Director Jerome Skolnick was funded under independent contract with the Commission, although he maintained close liaison with central office staff and with some study teams. To Skolnick, the advantages of this arrangement included insulation "from the time-consuming crises of Washington" and an independence of operation that was permitted by his contract with the Commission. Although I echo and admire these judgments, I am sure he would endorse the importance of having social scientists at the central office.

I fully supported the lawyer–social scientist team approach to task force operation, but by any standard, the most smoothly functioning task forces were those headed solely by academics (History and Comparative Perspectives, and Group Violence, or solely by lawyers (Law and Law Enforcement [after an initial period of indecision and lack of progress], and Firearms). The special investigative teams were, or appeared to be, similarly efficient in carrying out their assignments.

All working groups have problems; this was no less true of the task forces and special team (or for that matter, of the Short-Wolfgang collaboration), which were led solely by academics or by lawyers, than of the mixed groups. Several months into the effort, for example, leadership of the Law and Law Enforcement Task Force was transferred from one group of lawyers to another. The reason: despite a large-scale, and by-and-large successful, effort to recruit research and position papers on a variety of topics (The Commission's *Progress Report* listed thirty-six projects that were either completed or underway) little progress was being made toward completion of the task force report or of a statement on this topic for consideration by the Commission. But all of these groups were able to complete their assignments in reasonably good time and without personal acrimony. This was not true of the mixed leadership groups.

No simple diagnosis of the "root problems" of staff operation will do. Basic differences in perspective often characterized task force operation, with the lawyers tending more toward their customary posture of advocacy, marshaling available information in support of a particular position, and the social scientists wanting to look at "all sides of all questions" and most of all to generate new and specifically relevant data. Faced with such complex problems, however, positions of advocacy were in most cases not clear. In most instances, lawyers and social scientists joined freely in discussions of what information was needed and who could best be recruited to do the job, or what types of new data were needed. The list of social scientist consultants to the Commission is impressive in both its quality and its length.

In retrospect, although the lawyer–social scientists collaboration offers special problems, these can be and often are overcome. The difficulties attending such collaboration on the Violence Commission staff, I believe, had more to do with the enormous pressures associated with a very tight time schedule, with the lack of clear lines of authority and division of labor that characterized some task forces, and with the quite understandable desires of all participants to perform satisfactorily under these conditions. Occasional problems arose as a result of "personality clashes," and of ambitions (or pretentions) that exceeded capabilities. But these are hardly unique to the Commission form of doing things. And it would be unwise to dwell upon them for they distort as much as they inform the enterprise. There were good times, too, and staff morale generally was high during those early days. Many people gave unstintingly of their time and resources in the effort to get the job done.

THE SPECIAL INVESTIGATIVE STUDY TEAMS

The original organization of the Commission staff changed in response to a variety of circumstances. Even as the Commission was developing its plan of operation and preparing for hearings and staff recruitment continued, the dramatic events at the Democratic National Convention in Chicago forced a change in plans. The Commission made the decision to appoint a special study team to investigate the Chicago disorders. To balance matters politically, a second team was appointed to study the "ghetto riots" that had erupted in Miami at the time of the Republican Convention. Additionally, the Commission had been requested to support an ongoing study of the July 1968, shoot-out between police and black militants in Cleveland: in September the principal investigators of that study were appointed directors of a study team for that purpose. A fourth study team was appointed to investigate the disturbances then taking place at San Francisco State College, as a special opportunity for Commission study of campus-related violence. Finally, following release of *Rights in Conflict*, the dramatic Walker Report (after its chairman) on the violence at the Democratic National Convention, the relatively peaceful counterinaugural demonstrations attending President Nixon's inauguration were chosen for special study by the Task Force on Law and Law Enforcement.

The special study teams operated more independently of the Commission and its senior staff than did the task forces, and they were not integrated into the pattern of hearings and other Commission meetings which developed to consider the work of the latter. Like the task forces, however, and with the exception of the Cleveland study team (which had earlier been supported by the National Institute of Mental Health and the Lemberg Center for the Study of Violence at Brandeis University), all of these study teams were headed by lawyers. And with the exception of the young staff lawyer who wrote *Rights in Concord*, the counterinaugural demonstration report, all were men of stature in their communities, and in some cases, nationally. In this respect they were similar to the senior staff, or to the Commissioners. Daniel Walker, now Governor of Illinois, for example, was general counsel for Montgomery Ward and President of the Chicago Crime Commission. William H. Orrick, Jr., Director of the San Francisco State College Study Team, had been associated with the Kennedy administration and was head of a special San Francisco Crime Commission.

Appointment of the study teams was a delicate matter for the Commission. Events in Chicago had embarrassed the Democratic party and perhaps seriously damaged their election chances. The Commission felt compelled to investigate what had happened, but it recognized many dangers. Not only the choice of Walker as Director of the Chicago Study Team, but also negotiations with him were carried out with the utmost

secrecy. I learned of Walker's selection when I was called early one morning and invited to have breakfast with Walker, Cutler, and Campbell,
prior to a press conference at which announcement of the decision was
to be made. The fact that I was frustrated and disappointed not to have
been consulted in the matter is less important than is the insight into the
informal mode of Commission operation which is provided by the incident. I offered to help in any way possible, specifically, by suggesting
names of sociologists who might be helpful in the conduct of the investigation and to contact them. Little came of the effort. Walker organized a
massive investigative group, which functioned independently of other
Commission activities. The study team's efforts were spectacularly successful, as evidenced by "cover story" treatment in national magazines,
newspapers, and other media.

   Rights in Conflict is a classic documentation of problems related to
dissent in a free society, and particularly of police handling of mass demonstrations and protest activities. In the present context, however, the report's shortcomings are of greater interest than are its strengths because
they related to the Commission form of study. The report was researched
and written in the incredibly short time of fifty-three days, from September 27 to November 18, 1968. Several methods of investigation were followed, including access to thousands of FBI statements, news stories, and
photographs. Perhaps the major investigative technique, however, was to
seek sworn depositions from eyewitnesses. This technique, plus the un-
founded but understandable suspicion of many participants that a government "whitewash" was in the making—or worse yet, arrest and prosecution of demonstrators—led many participants (and potential informants)
to be uncooperative with the investigation. At several universities, for
example, study team investigators found few who would testify.

   Focus on eyewitness depositions led to another problem; that of the
failure to devote sufficient attention to the decisions of those under whose
auspices the police functioned. The latter problem was not ignored, for
the Report noted Mayor Daley's rebuke of police handling of riots in Chicago following the assassination of Martin Luther King, and the subsequent police violence directed against "demonstrators, bystanders, and
media representatives at a Civil Center peace march."[8] Mayor Daley la-

   [8]Daniel Walker. *Rights in Conflict, Report to the National Commission on the Causes
and Prevention of Violence* (New York: Bantam Books, 1968).

ter modified his "shoot to kill arsonists and shoot to maim looters" order on the first occasion, but police attacks at the peace march were officially ignored. Walker's team attempted to follow the complicated chronology of events leading to and during the violence of convention week in Chicago, but high-level involvement and decision-making were not systematically documented or researched at the "eyewitness" level. The police—surely culpable in view of what happened—bore the burden of responsibility just as surely shared by their civilian superiors. Thus, the pressure of time and the focus and methods of investigation led to an incomplete picture of those who participated in the violence (police and demonstrators) and of those who, in a larger sense, were responsible for the confrontation.

Appointment of other study teams also was closely guarded and carefully negotiated, although the results were less sensational. Again, we made some efforts to aid those teams, but our efforts were directed primarily toward coordinating and in other ways promoting the work of the task forces.

OF TIME AND CRISES

In his testimony before the Special Studies Subcommittee of the House Committee on Government Operations, approximately six months after the Commission had submitted its Final Report, Executive Director Lloyd Cutler noted that the eighteen months of the Commission's life was substantially longer than we had been anticipating. The role of social scientists in the Commission's work was greatly effected both by the original and final timing of Commission effort. The Executive Order creating the Commission specified its life as one year from the date of appointment, June 10, 1968. Because President Johnson was to go out of office early in 1969, it was requested that the Commission submit a report of progress prior to the inauguration of a new president. The Commission agreed to this request and scheduled and completed the primary staff efforts within six months. But, since most of the first two months were taken up by staff organization and the Academic Conference, the staff effort was even more highly concentrated, roughly from late July until early December, when the Commission met to hammer out the Progress Report. Furthermore, it was during that first six-month period that nineteen

full days of hearings and another conference—all requiring enormous ex
penditures of staff time and energy—were held.

The impact of timing effected individual Task Forces in different
ways. Skolnick was well organized and funded by the end of July, as were
Graham and Gurr and Newton and Zimring. Their reports on historical
and comparative perspectives, group violence, and firearms were the first
to be published. But I was still recruiting staff for the Task Force on Assassinations and Political Violence, and Law and Law Enforcement after the
ASA and Democratic National Conventions (which coincided that year).

Most recruitment of staff and persons to prepare papers for task
forces occurred in late July and August. Because the academic community
is poorly organized to respond quickly to external demands of any sort,
this process was less structured and more spontaneous than most large-
scale scholarly efforts. We started with names we knew to be expert in
certain areas, but we were forced to be opportunists. And with such enormous tasks to be completed in so short a time, quality control was difficult
to maintain.

The atmosphere of Commission activity is difficult to approximate
or imagine. In addition to recruiting task force directors, contributors,
and other consultants, the research directors met often with other members of the senior staff (executive and deputy directors, general counsel,
and administrative officer), individually and in various combinations. We
met often with task force directors and their consultants. We answered
hundreds of inquiries and suggestions from Congressmen, scholars, and
citizens who wrote to the Commission. We lunched and dined and met
at all hours among ourselves and with dozens of others. We counseled
on needed research and how to do it, on data reduction and interpretation, on budgets and payrolls, on hearings as well as documents, on public
relations. We helped organize and participated in hearings, and we per-
formed countless other tasks associated with the enterprise. We traveled
(Wolfgang back and forth across the Atlantic, I to New York to view hours
of film and video tape of the Democratic National Convention, which had
not been shown on television; to Chicago to see Walker and his crew; and
to Pullman, Washington to mend home fences). We also tried to keep up
with our non-Commission commitments. For example, I made a site visit
to an NIMH Training Grant Committee and attended meetings of the
Research Council of the National Council on Crime and Delinquency.

Finallly, there was an active social life—among Commissioners, between Commissioners and staff, and within the staff.

We worked incredibly long hours. Task Forces were under constant review by the senior staff. Task Force staffs were just as busy. The only full-time social scientist, Task Force co-director in the Washington office, Sandra Ball-Rokeach, estimates she spent at least 60 percent of her time on activities not directly related to research or report preparation.

While all of this activity seemed to occur more-or-less continuously in a frenetic melange, it was not unstructured. Staff contact with Commissioners, individually and collectively, was handled through the executive director, often with the assistance of the general counsel. Research directors were the chief mediators between task forces and senior staff, though there was much direct contact among all parties.

Mr. Cutler divides the work of the Commission into three distinct six-month periods. Most of what I have been describing took place during the first six months, which ended with the Commission's *Progress Report* drafted in December 1968, and submitted to President Johnson on January 9, 1969. It was during this period that a "research presence" was most conspicuous and most effective in the Commission's activities. Most of the research of all of the task forces was completed during this period, and in the *Progress Report*, the basic outlines of the Commission report became clear. After December 1968, I returned to Washington State University, though I traveled frequently to Washington, D.C. throughout the winter and spring of 1969. Wolfgang continued his occasional trips across the Atlantic. We both attended many meetings of the Commission, and we continued to confer with task force leaders whose reports had not been completed. But the continuous contact of researchers with lawyers and Commissioners and of research directors with task force researchers, which was characteristic of the first six months, never existed thereafter. During the second six months and into the third, we received drafts of Commission statements (usually prepared by the executive director and the general counsel, with important input by professional writers and staff researchers), but we were unable to keep up. From the beginning, the Commission had been plagued by fiscal difficulties, and funds for travel and consultation became scarce after the first six months. We continued to correspond with task force directors and to try to help them, but our attention was by then distracted by our other activities.

Crises

Crises—minor and major—played an important role in shaping the work of the Commission. I will briefly describe four crises and how they were resolved. In three of the four, the lawyer–social scientist division of labor proved something of a problem.

Hearings. One of the first points of contention between the researchers and the lawyers and Commissioners concerned the question of hearings. The senior staff lawyers and the Congressional members of the Commission insisted on public hearings. The research directors very early decided that since hearings would be a diversion from our primary task and productive of little new information, they therefore should not be held, particularly in view our our severe time limitations. We were overruled, however, and nineteen days of hearings were held between September 18 and December 20. These involved considerable planning and hard work by each of the task forces and they were agonizingly diverting. The hearings served at least three important purposes:

1   They provided a forum—often dramatic—for staff to bring points of view to the Commission. Skolnick refers to communication through emotional engagement as the "ultimate art" of "social science as theater."[9]
2   The hearings were a quick way to confront the Commissioners with information and points of view before task forces were ready with systematic information and analysis. The Commission thus got an early start in deliberation.
3   Most of the hearings were public, and they were well covered by the media. The Commission's activities thus received invaluable public attention to the problems they were studying.

Except for the last purpose, other formats probably would have been at least as effective as the hearings and probably less diverting for the staff. The conferences with university presidents, which were held in the spring of 1969, for example, were efficient and effective. But no such con-

[9]Jerome H. Skolnick. "The Violence Commission: Internal Politics and Public Policy," in *The Use and Abuse of Social Science,* edited by Irving Louis Horowitz, (:
Transaction Books, 1970.)

ferences were held with student leade s, antiwar protestors, or black militants. A conference on Youth and Violence gave substance to some of these interests, and the hearings provided a dramatic public forum, but neither of these proved adequate for detailed presentations and consideration of points of view or of systematic evidence. Few of the Commissioners attended the Conference on Youth and Violence and staff participation was limited largely to the Task Force that had planned it.

The first set of hearings was devoted to presentation of basic disciplinary perspectives on and dimensions of violence, at which several sociologists gave testimony. Wolfgang and I were at times given an opportunity to question those who appeared. None of the participating social scientists with whom I have talked about the matter have expressed satisfaction with the hearings' mode of inquiry.

Funding.   In his congressional testimony of May 1970, Mr. Cutler stated that one of the main problems of Presidential Commissions is obtaining funds:

> . . . Lacking direct appropriations sufficient to support its array of advisory commissions, the White House staff is in the difficult and demeaning position of having to beg the established departments for contributions which they are naturally reluctant to make in view of their own budgetary constraints. Through no fault of the individuals involved but simply because of the way the system now works, much lost time and strained relationships result from the series of financial crises through which a Presidential Commission routinely passes in the effort to do its job.

Funding was an especially acute problem for the Violence Commission, in part because the power of the Johnson administration to control funds was severely diminished during this "lame duck" period. Funding was hardly "routine" for staff whose livelihood was at stake. At one point, the Commission appeared on the verge of pulling out all together, and the staff was put on notice that their jobs might terminate at any moment. The strategy, if it was that, worked, for we did then receive funds. But the tension generated was excruciating, exacerbating the already existing strain among staff.

Funding, like time, received priority allocation. Several task forces decided they required original research. Considerable resistance to proposed new research was at first voiced by other members of the senior staff, ostensibly on the basis of reported experience with original research by other Commissions. However, by persisting in the argument that existing information in a number of areas was so inadequate that the task forces would be severely handicapped without new data, we did succeed in gaining funds. Several large-scale projects were carried out, including a national survey of adults concerning experiences with and attitudes toward violence, media preferences and practices; political beliefs and activities, and gun ownership; detailed content analysis of television entertainment programming for two successive years; special tabulations of FBI statistics and original surveys of police data for several cities; and trends in types of group violence as measured by newspaper coverage. Funds for these studies, and for support of ongoing research by consultants who contributed papers to the Commission efforts came both from governmental and foundation sources.

The Walker Report.   Even before the report of the Chicago Study Team had been submitted to the Commission, it became a problem. The report was a sensational indictment of official handling of the demonstrations at the Democratic National Convention, and particularly of police overreaction. There was considerable debate among both Commission and staff as to how to treat the report. The debate was quickly resolved, however, when it was discovered that *LIFE* magazine was planning a cover story based on the report in a matter of days. There was much discussion as to the source of the "leak" but the Commission quickly authorized public release of the report so as to beat the "scoop." The publicity following the report once again placed the Commission in the public spotlight and gave broader voice to staff and commission findings alike.

The Politics of Protest.   Jerome Skolnick substituted his discussion of the Violence Commission, "Internal Politics and Public Policy." He referred to the Commissioners as the primary audience of his task force, although he acknowledged that "In the long run, the university had to be our major audience, since the report is scholarly and the media treated its publication as news, quickly displaced by other stories."[10] His assessment of audience priorities is probably typical of the attitude with which

[10]Ibid., p. 24.

academics approach service on Commissions. We continue to write primarily for each other and for our students, perhaps out of the conviction that what we have to say will not be listened to for ideological reasons, perhaps because we are advisedly less certain of our data and interpretations than the Commissioners (or policy-makers) would like us to be. Skolnick appears convinced of the former, while I am inclined toward the latter as an "explanation," although ideological gaps are often undeniable. In any case, he attempted to convince the Commission of the task force point of view.

The approach taken by the Task Force on Group Violence was to emphasize "social history and political analysis," and this did, indeed, "violate some of the expectations of some portions of our audience," notably the Commissioners.[11] The Commission felt that the task force report presented an interpretation and a series of conclusions, instead of carrying out its assignment to provide the facts necessary to reach a conclusion. There is some justification to this charge. As the *Report* notes, it "is not an investigation, it is an analysis." The lack of more data, understandable in view of the crush of time, left "an enormous gap in research—in factual information," as Dr. Eisenhower explained to me. In the end, the Commission rejected the analysis and substituted its own, based largely on materials from the Task Force on Historical and Comparative Perspectives and the several special study teams. The Commission decision was based as much on ideological differences with the *Report* as upon the lack of an adequate factual base, but the latter could be pointed to as the basis for decision.

The Commission felt it necessary to emphasize the necessity for more adequate control measures as well as for attention to the "root causes" of violence—a position deliberately eschewed by the task force on the grounds that such recommendations were likely to result in more control as a substitute for addressing basic social injustices.

Both points of view were published. The Commission made no attempt to suppress the *Task Force Report,* but it hardly acknowledged it in its own *Final Report.* Suppression of task force reports would, in any case, have been virtually impossible as a result of a freedom-to-publish agreement, which we obtained from the Commission. Under that agreement, all task force reports were required to be submitted to the Commis-

11Ibid.

sion, which had the option of publishing or releasing them to the task force directors, who could make their own publication arrangements. In the end, the Commission decided to publish all task force reports as reports "to the Commission," but with neither endorsement nor disclaimer. Several of the reports were subsequently published by private publishers, some with additional editorial work and commentary by task force directors.

A Final Note on the Report of the Task Force on Group Violence

Although I cannot document this specifically, I believe that considerable support existed among both staff and commissioners for the Report's interpretation, as distinguished from the recommendations that attention should be focused on root causes rather than strengthening of the criminal justice system. There was also considerable criticism of portions of the methodology and interpretation in the report among our academic advisors, some of which has been aired in scholarly publications. In the end, the Report proved too controversial to "make it" in the Commission's Report, but it remains an important contribution to the literature.

WINDING UP

The first report to the Commission was the Walker Report, on November 18, 1968. The next, also a Special Study Team Report (Shootout in Cleveland), was not published until May 1969. The Politics of Protest quickly followed, as did the reports on Firearms and on San Francisco State College. It was not until the fall of 1969, between October and December, after many trials, that the final task force volumes were published.

The Commission's Progress Report marked the high point of social science input to the Commission. That report followed the period of most intensive staff activity during which hearings were held, literature surveyed and research generated, and preliminary task force reports prepared. Following distribution of the preliminary reports, Commissioners met for three days in early December with senior staff to discuss each report with task force directors and to draft the Commission's preliminary report. Discussion at that meeting was lively, provocative, and productive.

I wish more people would read that report. Despite compromises, we were able to secure Commission endorsement of our neutral definition of violence and of several "themes of challenge": including the *relativity* of attributions of legitimacy or illegitimacy to violence; the essentially social (as opposed to biological or psychological) nature of most violence; the essential connection between perceived legitimacy of the law and effective legal control of violence; the fundamental notion of "relative deprivation" (though we did not call it that); and the notion that responsibility for violence often lies in the unresponsiveness of social institutions. The progress reports of the task forces that were published together with the Commission statement reflected more fully the task force perspectives than did the Commission *Final Report*.

Following the December Conference, the staff never again assembled for such a meeting. Task force directors met with Commissioners for discussion of their reports and as an aid in preparation of the Commission's statements. Wolfgang and I attended several of these meetings, but my own direct contact with the Commissioners tapered off rapidly and I never met with them after the spring of 1969. From my limited contacts, I can testify that these meetings were also lively, and that task force directors did an excellent job in presenting their materials. I could cite specific instances where staff findings changed Commission perceptions of a problem and others where such materials were ineffective. Overall, I am convinced that the basic needs of our discipline are compatible with the needs of Commissions; that is, both require more and better data, and data and analysis that are relevant to policy issues and responsive to problems in the real world.

The final six months of the Commission's life was marked by the release of a series of statements which later became chapters in the final report. The first, an "Interim Statement on Campus Disorder," was issued on June 9, 1969. Because that statement was well received both within and outside of government, it became, as Cutler testified in May 1970, "something of a turning point in the life of the Commission . . . it persuaded the Commission to adopt a policy of serial release of a number of separate statements rather than the single release of one final report."

Following release of the first statement, the Commission was informed by the Nixon White House staff that it should proceed with future releases without the necessity for prior White House clearance. This set the pattern. A second statement, concerning "Firearms and Violence," was issued on July 28, and a third, on "Violence in Television Entertainment Programs," on September 23. Remaining statements, commencing with "Violence and Law Enforcement" on November 1, were issued more rapidly as the Commission's work was drawing to a close. By December 1969, a year after the major staff effort was completed, a total of eight statements had been issued and given national coverage by the media. "Thereafter," again quoting Mr. Cutler's testimony, "the Commission swiftly and unanimously reached agreement on the fundamental conclusion drawn from its study—that the causes of violence are deeply rooted in our institutional failures to correct social injustices as well as in weaknesses of the law enforcement system, and that the prevention of violence required a two-pronged approach aimed at making resort to violence unnecessary as well as unrewarding." The Commission's *Final Report* was submitted to the President on December 10, 1969, the expiration date of its extended life.

During the last six months of Commission activity, the burden of writing and staff liaison fell increasingly on the shoulders of General Counsel James Campbell and a few professional writers who had been recruited to complete the effort. By this time, though occasional letters continued to flow across the country, the research team, dissipated and spent, had little interaction with the Commission, and the research directors little with personnel of the task forces whose reports were as yet incomplete.

ON SCHOLARSHIP, RECOMMENDATIONS, AND IMPACT

The Commission's final report includes eighty-one recommendations, beginning with the pronouncement that "the time is upon us for a reordering of national priorities and for a greater investment of resources in the fulfillment of two basic purposes of our constitution—to establish justice and to insure domestic tranquility" and ending with the admonition "that all our citizens, young and old, try to bridge the 'generation gap.' " Vague prescriptions such as these were supported by equally broad, but somewhat more specific recommendations; for example, the proposal that general welfare expenditures be increased and military expenditures reduced or kept level (in constant dollars). Many of the recommendations reiterate those made by previous commissions (e.g., those concerned with crime, civil disorders, and reform of the draft system). Others urge more effective implementation of goals specified in existing legislation; for example, the 1968 Housing Act ("a decent home for every American within a decade") and the Employment Act of 1946 ("a useful job for all who are able to work"). Others were more specific, for example, that "the Constitution of the United States be amended to lower the voting age for all state and federal elections to eighteen," and extension of the Gun Control Act of 1968 "to prohibit domestic production and sale of 'junk guns.' "

Special attention was devoted to urban problems, including a proposal advocated by the Executive Director that "the President . . . convene an urban convention of delegates from all states and major cities, as well as the national government, to advise the nation on the steps that should be taken to increase efficiency and accountability through structural changes in local government."

Further research was called for at several points and "to aid in the reordering of national priorities." Approval was given to "a counterpart of the Council of Economic Advisors to develop tools for measuring the comparative effectiveness of social programs, and to produce an Annual Social Report comparable to the present Annual Economic Report."

It seems a fair assessment to say that the Commission's recommendations were liberal but unexceptional. Little that was new was added to analyses and proposals already before the public, in one form or another. It deliberately sought to avoid identification of the Commission position with catch phrases such as the "white racism" label which so dominated the public image of the Kerner Commission. A task force report at one point, for example, described the accumulation of firearms in urban areas as "an urban arms race." The phrase (quite rightly, I believe), was objected to by the Commission as too sensational and uninformative and it was excised from the final task force reports.

In every case, however, the Commission listened to, discussed, and debated the task force reports before issuing their own statements. Their posture tended to be more cautious than that advocated by the task forces, but they were heavily influenced by the latter, even when they rejected them, as in the case of the Task Force on Group Violence. That debate was often instructive. I recall a long afternoon of Commission deliberation concerning a preliminary report of the Task Force on Law and Law Enforcement in which several Commissioners, including the chairman, voiced their failure to understand why all citizens did not have the faith they shared in our system of law and justice. At this point, evidence on the distribution of answers to political efficacy questions from the

Commission-sponsored national survey was introduced. That evidence pointed so overwhelmingly to the association of affluence, advanced educational status, and majority status with high political efficacy; and its converse, the association of poverty, the lack of education, and minority status with low political efficacy, that some Commissioners at least were convinced. The gap between "professed ideals and actual performance," the idealism that often motivates collective violence, the pervasive influence of violence in American history, including the role of police and others interested in preserving the status quo, and including "positive effects" of collective violence, the high incidence of exposure to and participation in violence by contemporary Americans, and the perversion of the rule of law by television entertainment programming—those and many more aspects of violence in this society, brought to their attention by staff reports, influenced what the Commission thought and did. They were not always convinced, and their *Final Report* is carefully couched so as not to be politically offensive (e.g., questioning the subordination of general welfare to national defense expenditures, but calling for a reversal of this relationship "when our participation in the Vietnam War is concluded," rather than confronting the analysis of the effects of that war that was provided in staff reports). Perhaps because they were concerned to achieve consensus among themselves, perhaps due to the press of external demands (e.g., from the President or their own constituencies, or their desire to bring about consensus among a badly divided American public), anomalies occur in the Commission's *Report*. Despite evidence of vast differences in political and economic power among segments of the population, and much sophistication among Commissioners and senior staff in the operation of interest group politics, for example, the statement is made that "national priorities reflect the value judgments of the majority." Staff reports repeatedly note institutional aspects of violence, but the Commission *Report* seems insensitive to the role of conflict in institutional functioning. Yet is is sensitive to the importance of institutional legitimacy, including the very foundation of the rule of law.

Impact

The Commission's work received more than the usual amount of national publicity accorded such matters, in part because of the policy of holding press conferences and releasing statements as they were developed, rather than waiting for completion of the *Final Report*. Additionally, the Commission and its director had exceptionally good connections with the mass media. Commission statements, portions of the public hearings, and several of the task force reports were well publicized. The Commission's *Final Report*, at least three Task Force Reports *(The Politics of Protest, Violence in America,* and *Law and Order Reconsidered),* and two of the Special Study Team Reports *(Rights in Conflict* and *Shoot-Out in Cleveland)* were published commercially in addition to U.S. Government Printing Office distribution. These reports, in paperback, were widely displayed in bookstores, airports, and other public places.

Other types of follow-up were planned. National Organizations endorsed the Commission's work, and the National Council on Crime and Delinquency and the Anti-Defamation League distributed (under their imprimatur) copies of the eighty-one Commission recommendations. Plans were made for a national committee of prominent persons to be chaired by an eminent university president, to promote achievement of those recommendations, similar to the group formed to oversee recommendations, and follow up the analysis, of the National Advisory Commission on Civil Disorders. For reasons unknown to me, this plan never was implemented.

Although the impact of dramatic publicity may be fleeting, its importance should not be discounted. The drama of Chicago in 1968 was later reinforced by the *Walker Report*. More importantly, the *Walker Report* is an important part of the greatly expanded literature of political sociology, as are other Commission documents. Impact must also be assessed on the basis of actions and in the longer run. I know of no specific Congressional action flowing from the work of the Violence Commission, but its work is a part of the record of that body. The reports of the Commissions and its staff have been widely used in college classrooms and in some high schools. In some instances additional research articles and volumes following up that work have been published by Commission staff members or consultants; see, for example, articles by Campbell, Currie and Skolnick, Graham, Gurr, Levy, McEvoy, Neiburg, Rossie and Berke, Smelser, and Short and Wolfgang in the September 1970, issue of *The Annals of the American Academy of Political and Social Science;* also, the chapter by Ball-Rokeach and the expanded chapter by Short and Wolfgang in the

book that grew out of that issue[12] and Horowitz.[13] Other work has analyzed various aspects of the Commission's efforts, including innumerable
reviews (Platt, 1971; Grimshaw, 1971; Quinney, 1971). Reviews and
other commentary have not always been complimentary; nor should they
be. The important point is that the Commission's work has become a part
of critical scholarly discourse.

Behavioral effects of Commission scholarship and recommendations
are difficult and probably impossible to measure in any systematic way.
Anecdotal evidence is suspect on several counts, but it sometimes is the
best we have. I am aware of an event that points up both the initial failure
of governmental agencies to act intelligently upon Commission evidence
and recommendations, and the eventual "success" of such action once
undertaken. In the fall of 1969, less than a year after publication of *Rights
in Conflict, Violence in America, The Politics of Protest,* and *Rights in
Concord,* the refusal of the Justice Department to grant parade permits
to peace groups for a silent march around the White House in protest
against the war in Indochina was widely publicized. Extensive media publicity and personal contact with the White House by a Commission representative, pointing out the incongruity of the refusal to grant the requested permits with Violence Commission evidence concerning such
matters, led to a reversal of the Justice Department's action. The permits
were issued and the march, held in November 1969, took place without
incident—further evidence of "Rights in Concord."

CONCLUSION

As sociologists, we ought to organize ourselves better to respond to the
national interest, as I have broadly defined it (see footnote 1). I think we
can do this through the American Sociological Association: its Executive
Office should be a clearinghouse for persons with particular talents and
interests, for both the Congress and the executive and judicial branches
of government and for other institutions, when sociological expertise is
needed. The Executive Office now serves this function willy-nilly, as do

[12]James F. Short, Jr. and Marion E. Wolfgang. *Collective Violence* (Chicago: Aldine-
Altherton, 1972).

[13]Irving Louis Horowitz. *The Struggle is the Message: the Organization and Ideology
of the Anti-War Movement* (Berkeley: the Glendessary Press, 1970).

many individual sociologists, when we are called upon. But this is not enough. The Association has moved in recent years toward more systematic attention to the needs of women and minorities within the profession and in our relations with non-sociologists. We must give more attention to broadening the external relations aspects of this concern to the entire profession—in the interests of the profession, the discipline, and the national interest. The potential ramifications for each are great. The task should not be taken lightly, for it will require the highest degree of statesmanship and sociological wisdom.

I am acutely conscious of the charges and problems related to co-optation of scholars and scholarship, of the "cooling the public out" functions of Commissions and other study groups, and of legitimizing by our participation particular political policies and governments. But these same arguments can be turned around. We also co-opt; indeed, my argument is that we should be more attentive to doing so. Our research is supported and we bring our scholarly efforts to a far broader audience when they are attended by the sponsorship and publicity accorded national commissions. Those efforts can be made to serve the traditional scholarly function of critical evaluation of institutions, including governments. The fact that the reports of so many recent national commissions have been forcefully, or by silence and neglect, repudiated by national leaders in both executive and legislative branches of government suggests we have not been altogether unsuccessful in the latter respect. My argument is that we can do more, and do it more effectively. Failure to participate can lead only to less impact. I am frank to admit that I was naive and unprepared for many aspects of the Violence Commission experience. I learned a great deal, but service on a national commission is not a very good setting for on-the-job training, if one is interested in results. The implications seem clear, if not specific. We need to be much more skilled, we need much more highly developed data bases, and we need organization and sophistication in matters of government and the law if we are to be more effective.

CHAPTER FOUR

Report On the President's Commission On Law Enforcement And Administration Of Justice

LLOYD E. OHLIN

Harvard Law School

On July 23, 1965, by executive order, President Lyndon Johnson established the Commission on Law Enforcement and the Administration of Justice. I served on the staff of the Commission as an Associate Director in charge of the Task Force on Assessment of the Crime Problem. There were no other sociologists on the Commission or in senior staff positions.

ORIGINS OF THE NATIONAL CRIME COMMISSION

There were many events that led to the establishment of the National Crime Commission—some precipitous, some peripheral. The assassinations of Martin Luther King and John F. Kennedy shocked the nation and brought the issue of violence to the foreground of public attention. Public opinion polls showed a rise in citizen concern and anxiety about the increasing violence within our society and the violence attending our commitments in Southeast Asia. The harsh and bloody confrontations of the civil rights demonstrations in the South were spreading to the urban ghettos of the North. And the rise in crime rates throughout the nation—not only in urban areas, but rural and surburban communities as well— steadily heightened the fears of citizens regarding the safety of their persons and property.

This increasing public preoccupation with the sources and consequences of violence was reflected in the presidential campaign of 1964. The Republicans, led by Senator Barry Goldwater, attacked the administration's failure to cope with the burgeoning violence: they charged that the permissiveness and "socialist-minded" doctrines of the Democratic administration undermined respect for law and order. The attack focused on "crime in the streets" as a coded slogan for all types of violent conduct, particularly the growing turbulent unrest and public protests of minority groups (i.e., blacks and radical activists) in both the South and the North.

By the summer of 1965, it became apparent that the Great Society programs launched by President Johnson in the so-called war on poverty were doing as much to exacerbate as to alleviate these tensions and confrontations. Increasing commitment to the war in Vietnam added to the prevailing public levels of concern about violence. Some type of Presidential initiative seemed necessary to deal directly with the issue of "crime in the streets." Sociologists had been active during the presidential campaign, developing data and analyses for the Johnson candidacy to show that street crimes were being dealt with by increasing commitment of resources through the Great Society programs, and that fears of crime were being inflated for political purposes. Councillors to the President advised positive steps to deal with this problem so that it would not remain a viable issue in the elections of 1968.

Yet it was not clear what types of federal action should be taken. Traditionally, the problem of crime and its control had been defined as a state and local, rather than a federal, responsibility. The federal government had the responsibility to maintain a system of law enforcement, prosecution, judicatory, and correctional services to deal with violation of federal laws. But the prototypical "crime in the street," involving assault or threat of violence at the hands of a stranger, almost always fell under the jurisdiction of state and local laws and enforcement agencies. For many years, Congress had resisted efforts to fund crime prevention and control programs to assist the states and local communities. Under strong pressure during the early years of the Kennedy administration, this resistance had weakened to permit the passage of federal delinquency legislation in support of states and local communities in 1961. This, however, was only a small program, which involved appropriations of $6 to $8 million a year, devoted primarily to aiding a number of cities to develop community delinquency prevention programs for youth. Therefore, in the summer of 1965, there was uncertainty as to what form a bold federal initiative to deal with crime in the streets might take without risking a charge of excessive encroachment by the federal government on state and local responsibilities. A Presidential Commission seemed to be an acceptable beginning. There was sufficient time for such a commission to do its work and for legislation to be developed and passed—prior to the elections of 1968. Such a commission with a broad mandate could search out the best advice at national, state, and local levels: it could formulate recommendations for action that would achieve widespread support in Congress and elsewhere.

From the beginning, the charge to the Commission was pragmatic and remedial: the Commission should size up the dimensions of the problem and the sources of public fear; it should try to arrive at practical answers to the crime problem, which could be implemented through legislation at federal, state, and local levels; and it should also recommend administrative measures to reform the system and effectively redistribute and reallocate both existing and newly committed resources. Thus the Commission was charged with inquiring into the causes of crime and delinquency and reporting back to the President, in eighteen months, with recommendations for preventing crime and delinquency and improving law enforcement and the administration of criminal justice.

The pervasive feeling among all those connected with the Commission was that the President's mandate contained a serious and responsible charge. The Commission was not designed solely as an expression of Presidential concern or as a diversionary political tactic: the political realities required a much more substantial federal commitment. The Commission had the responsibility of designing effective strategies for discharging that commitment. Its work, if well done, would find a receptive audience at the federal level, which was prepared to take action to commit new federal resources and initiatives to the problem.

THE STRUCUTURE OF THE COMMISSION

This interpretation of the Presidential mandate to the Commission is further reinforced by the President's actions in organizing the Commission. Instead of reaching out for an independent, prestigious chairman, the President chose to appoint his own Attorney General, Nicholas Katzenbach, as chairman of the Commission. Katzenbach had served as deputy attorney general during the Kennedy years and was appointed by Johnson to succeed Robert Kennedy as Attorney General. It seemed clear from the outset that the administration wished to retain considerable control to insure that the product of the Commission's work would provide achievable guidelines for federal action on the crime problem.

For executive director of the Commission, Katzenbach picked a personal friend, James Vorenberg, with whom he had worked closely on other occasions and whose judgment he trusted. Vorenberg was on leave from the Harvard Law School where he was a professor of law. He was directing the action-research program of the Office of Criminal Justice, a unit of the Department of Justice that had been created in 1963. For deputy director, Vorenberg appointed Henry Ruth, who had worked for a number of years in the organized crime section of the Department of Justice and most recently as an assistant to Vorenberg in the Office of Criminal Justice.

Additional evidence that the Presidential mandate was not reaching for new radical proposals for change in the criminal justice system was apparent from the composition of the Commission membership. Fifteen of the nineteen members (including the chairman) of the Commission were lawyers. The remaining four represented important constituencies. They included the chief of police of San Francisco, the publisher of the Los Angeles *Times*, the president of the League of Women Voters, and the executive director of the National Urban League. Among the lawyers, excluding the chairman, there were three judges, two prosecutors, three past presidents of the American Bar Association, the mayor of the city of New York, a former attorney general of the United States during the Eisenhower years, a close personal friend of the President, a member of a state board of pardons, and the highly respected reporter of the Model Penal Code for the American Law Institute.[1] In the main, then, the Com-

[1]The names and professional experience of the Commission members can be found in the general report of the Commission, *The Challenge of Crime in a Free Society*, (Washington, D.C.: U.S. Government Printing Office, 1967) Appendix A, pp. 309–311.

mission was composed primarily of lawyers whose considerable past experience in the private and public practice of law had earned national recognition for their legal accomplishments. This group was not likely to entertain radical critiques or drastic proposals for change in the existing criminal justice system. Their modes would be carefully documented, feasible proposals for reform designed to make the *existing* system work more effectively in prevention and control of crime. Recommendations that achieved the consensual support of such a Commission could be expected to carry great weight and gain wide acceptance.

At the outset the work of the Commission was organized into four task forces, with an associate director in charge of each. In naming the four associate directors, the executive director selected persons who could gain the confidence of the criminal justice constituency primarily represented by their task force: a state director of police training in California was chosen to head the Police Task Force; a young lawyer from New York with experience in trial practice was appointed as head of the Court Task Force; a former correctional administrator and professor of public administration from the University of Southern California was made head of the Corrections Task Force; and I was selected as a sociologist in charge of the Task Force on Assessment of The Crime Problem.[2] As the Commission work proceeded, a Task Force on Science and Technology was added through a contract with the Institute for Defense Analysis. In addition, several sub-task forces were organized to devote special attention to juvenile delinquency and youth crime, organized crime, narcotics and drug abuse, drunkenness offenses, control of firearms, and strategies for implementation of Commission recommendations.

Each of the major task forces and sub-task forces created their own technical advisory panel of experts. Staff members for the task forces were

[2]Since I was the only sociologist in a senior staff position on the Commission it might be useful to the analysts of this paper to know how I was selected to work on the Commission. At that time, I was a professor of sociology at the Columbia University School of Social Work and director of its research center. Most of my professional life had been devoted to studies of crime and criminal justice. During the 50's I served as an advisor to Professor Herbert Wechsler of Columbia University Law School and reporter for the Model Penal Code. During 1961–1962, while on leave of absence from Columbia University, I helped to organize the first federal program in delinquency as Special Assistant to Secretary Abraham Ribicoff in the U.S. Department of Health, Education and Welfare. Early in 1964, with Leonard S. Cottrell, Jr. of the Russell Sage Foundation and Joseph Dean of the School of Criminology at Berkeley, I headed a delegation to urge Attorney General Nicholas Katzenbach and James Vorenberg to begin the development of a National Institute of Criminal Justice to support more extensive research and demonstration projects in that field. I thus

hired by the task force directors with the approval of the executive director. Among the forty staff members of the Commission, not including secretarial and other support staff, there were two sociologists, both members of the Task Force on Assessment of the Crime Problem. In addition, there was one anthropologist and four social workers who had had sociological training. The remainder were young lawyers or young professionals with practical experience in criminal justice agencies.

The small number of sociologists was a matter of concern to me as well as to the executive director. The chief obstacle to recruiting knowledgeable sociologists as staff members was that recruitment began in October 1965, after the academic year was already underway. Academic and other professional or personal commitments prevented those invited from joining the Washington staff and from performing other than consultant roles. We were also unable to find sociologists with training in criminology in other government agencies who could be freed on loan to the Commission for the duration of its work. However, it did prove possible to secure the assistance of professionals in other government agencies for shorter periods of time, to prepare special reports or recommendations in the area of their expertise, such as juvenile delinquency, organized crime, narcotics and drug abuse, control of firearms, riot control, and implementation of Commission recommendations.

Sociologists contributed primarily as consultants and advisers. Consultants served on the technical advisory panels of the task forces or prepared papers under contract to the task force on special topics. Advisors included those who made less substantial commitments to the work of the Commission. The report of the Commission shows that there were 231 consultants involved in the Commission's work and 227 additional advisors.[3] Of the 231 consultants: 62 were sociologists and 27 were other social scientists such as economists, psychologists, and historians; 38 were lawyers; and 104 came from other professions, primarily experts in police,

---

had some prior acquaintance with the chief organizers of the Commission, though the invitation to join the Commission staff seemed to be based primarily on the recommendation of Professor Herbert Wechsler, whose judgment was highly regarded by Katzenbach and Vorenberg.

[3]These counts are rough approximations but probably fairly close. I tried to eliminate those listed more than once because they served in more than one task force as consultant or advisor. In some cases the professional identification was sketchy and the classification the best approximation possible. However, at least 90 percent of those classified as sociologists had Ph.D.'s in sociology.

courts, and corrections as well as physical scientists and engineers involved in the Science and Technology Task Force. Among the advisors there were a few additional sociologists and other social scientists.

The major contributions of social scientists to the Commission were made in their roles of consultants or advisors. Occasionally, these involved large contracts for research, which engaged the services of other sociologists not enumerated above. We shall return frequently to problems arising from this utilization of consultants as a primary source of social science information and recommendations for the final report of the Commission.

The Commission secured congressional appropriations totaling approximately $1,250,000. The Commission also received substantial help in launching research studies and surveys from the newly organized Office of Law Enforcement Assistance in the Department of Justice. This office was organized to provide support for research, demonstration projects, training programs, and technical assistance to federal and state law enforcement and criminal justice agencies. If these collaborative projects are included, approximately $2 million were spent in undertaking the work of the Commission. This does not include many expenditures by state and local criminal justice agencies or other federal departments who responded to inquiries from the Commission but were not directly compensated for their work.

HOW THE COMMISSION DID ITS WORK

The Commission met infrequently from July 23, 1965, to June 30 1967, when the Commission offices were finally closed. The full Commission met a total of seven times for periods of two or three days each, throughout the life of the Commission. These meetings occurred more frequently in the beginning when the work was being organized and more frequently near the end when final recommendations and reports required Commission approval. In addition, the Commission members were assigned special responsibilities to participate in different task forces as sub-panels. This device assured that at least some Commission members would be fully informed about the work of each of the task forces.

The first meeting of the Commission and key staff took place in September 1965, at which time basic decisions were made about the organization of the task forces and the scope of their work. By December 1965, detailed task force plans covering the scope and subjects of inquiry, issues where final recommendations should be reached, and a preliminary outline of the content of the final task force report were approved by the Commission.

In these early months, the staff was engaged in planning the work of the task forces, securing the services of consultants, and planning data-gathering processes. During the next phase, from January to June 1966, while consultant papers were being written, the staff was engaged in gathering statistics and other data, making field trips to observe criminal justice operations, and attending conferences and specially arranged meetings of interested groups to explain the work of the Commission in order to secure support and assistance wherever possible. Data and recommendations were also obtained from other federal agencies including the FBI, the Bureau of Prisons, the Criminal Division of the Department of Justice, several of the constituent agencies of the Department of Health, Education and Welfare, the Department of Labor, the Department of the Treasury, and the Bureau of the Budget. The Commission sponsored conferences on such matters as riots and their control, correctional standards, mentally disordered offenders, plea bargaining, and the federal role in crime control. One conference brought scientists and businessmen together to consider ways of working together against crime. Another inquired into the legal manpower problems of the criminal system. A third, in October 1966, was attended by representatives of the state committees appointed by many governors in response to the President's request that a group be formed in each state to plan and implement a reform of its criminal system and laws. In this connection, the Commission staff also worked with state and local criminal justice personnel to obtain information on the operation of their criminal justice systems and the likely effect of Commission proposals upon them.

By the summer of 1966, consultant papers were beginning to come in. Staff members were busy incorporating the results of these papers into reports and recommendations for the Commission's approval. During that summer, a few leading scholars from corrections, police work, and law came to Washington to work with the staff on a full-time basis, to develop these reports and recommendations. However, the principal role of most of the consultants was to serve as a sounding board for new ideas, proposed recommendations, and materials being developed for Commission consideration.

During the fall of 1966, staff and commission efforts greatly intensified to produce a final general report and set of recommendations. Many Commission members were consulted informally by staff as well as through the formally constituted sub-panels which sometimes included outside experts.

After much frantic effort on the part of staff and intense and sometimes heated discussions on controversial issues at Commission meetings, a final report was delivered to the President in January 1967, and published by the Government Printing Office in February 1967. Thereafter, the task force reports were given final approval and released as they became ready. By June 30, 1967, all of the nine task force and sub-task force reports had been released, in addition to the reproduction of a large number of consultant papers and field surveys undertaken for the Commission.

It should be clear from the foregoing account that the Commission gathered data from a wide variety of sources. The staff and the Commission relied heavily on information, opinions, and recommendations supplied by expert consultants and advisors. A determined effort was made to develop factual support for policies, general strategies, and specific recommendations. Much of this support came from statistics, studies, and documents available to criminal justice agencies or published in the literature. In addition, special field studies were undertaken. For example, with the collaboration and support of the Office of Law Enforcement Assistance, the Task Force on Assessment of the Crime developed contracts with NORC to undertake a national survey of unreported crime, the attitudes of both victims and the general public toward crime and criminal justice, and the measures taken in self-defense. Similar contracts were developed with the Bureau of Social Science Research in Washington and with the Michigan Survey Research Center to do more intensive studies of high-crime precincts in Washington, D.C., Chicago, and Boston. These surveys provided heretofore unavailable types of information for gauging public concern and fear about crime, the experiences of victims of crime, attitudes toward reporting of crime, and the measures citizens were taking to defend themselves.

Another survey, also the first of its kind, secured data on correctional personnel and facilities throughout the United States, in cooperation with the field staff of the National Council on Crime and Delinquency. Questionnaires were also sent to over 22,000 police departments throughout the country concerning the effectiveness of field procedures against crime. Field observers rode with the police and developed reports on citizen–police interactions. They also studied and observed procedures in the lower criminal courts. Staff members met with groups of residents in slum areas and with professional criminals and ex-offenders, to try to develop a more complete picture of the criminal justice system and its impact. In other words, the field studies undertaken by the Commission, its staff and consultants, constituted a valuable resource for filling gaps in existing knowledge about crime and the operation of the criminal justice system.

The type of information to be collected, the research studies to be done, and the consultants to be engaged were developed by the staff as part of each task force plan with the advice of Commission members and the technical advisory panels. These plans, which were regularly reviewed by the executive director, required advance approval and negotiation where contracts were being issued. The results of this information-gathering and research were assimilated into staff reports or summaries. When the research or consultant reports were especially helpful, they were distributed in their entirety to Commission members or to the task force Commission sub-panel.

Virtually all of the factual material reported to the Commission in one way or another became incorporated in the published reports of the various task forces. The opinions, speculations, and theories presented by the consultants were used where they seemed to enlarge understanding of the topics under consideration or sometimes to demonstrate the relatively unstructured and inconclusive state of theorizing in a particular field. Task force directors arranged the research contracts and chose consultants and research groups subject to the final approval of the executive director.

A great deal of consultation took place through the informal contacts that staff members had with colleagues in their own fields. The areas of knowledge of Commission members, staff, technical advisory panels, and consultants were constantly tapped to ensure that the Commission would not overlook valuable work going on elsewhere in the United States or in foreign countries. Repeatedly, as the reports took shape, gaps in information and understanding of the system were identified and new knowledge-generating processes were undertaken. For example, at one point the Assessment Task Force found it essential to develop better data on the economic costs of crime through intensive staff work. At one advanced stage in the development of the Police Task Force report, an intensive search was initiated for better data on the state of police–community relationships, especially in ghetto areas in large cities. The Corrections Task Force discovered the need tó develop better conceptualized models of alternative correctional practices. The Science and Technology Task Force tried to develop data on the costs to the system of processing different types of offenders over their lifetime criminal careers. Where conflicting evidence could not be reconciled through further inquiry, the conflicting data would often simply be reported as irreconcilable—beyond the capacity of the commission with its time and cost limitations to resolve.

There were times when the information developed proved too sensitive to be fully disclosed in the Commission's report. This was true, for example, in the area of organized crime, where access had been given staff members to confidential files maintained by state and local governments. The confidentiality of these files had to be respected to prevent premature disclosures adverse to successful prosecution. In such cases, staff could only report prevailing practices without full documentation.

Occasionally, information was inadvertently uncovered during the course of research studies that proved too embarrassing and difficult for the Commission to handle. A particularly notable illustration occurred during the research activities of a University of Michigan team under the direction of sociologist Albert J. Reiss, Jr. His observers rode in police cars in three cities and observed instances of police brutality and corruption, which were duly reported to the research files. However, the commitment of the research project to maintain the confidentiality of its informants prevented the publication of this material or identification of those involved. Members of the press learned that this evidence was available to Commission researchers and accused the Commission of suppression of important public information. This led to a wearying series of meetings, demands, and counterdemands that were never fully resolved during the life of the Commission. Professor Reiss has since published the results of his field observations in an article in *Transaction* and in a series of lectures at Yale University.[4] In the more recent as well as the earlier published accounts, however, the confidentiality of respondents was maintained. In the sensitive area of criminal justice, there is always great tension be-

[4]Albert J. Reiss, Jr., "Police-Brutality-Answers to Key Questions," *Transaction* 5 (July-August 1968): 15–16, and *The Police and the Public* (New Haven, Yale University Press, 1971).

tween the need to know for the purpose of developing knowledge and public policy and the need to know in order to prosecute wrongdoing. And the research worker is occasionally caught between these two conflicting purposes.

During the Commission's work, the Assessment Task Force was perceived as a major resource by other task forces for securing access to social science knowledge. Many of the research studies undertaken by the Assessment Task Force generated information which was then distributed to the other task forces for their use as it came in. The Assessment Task Force also helped to identify social scientists working in areas covered by the other task forces and assisted them in contracting consultant and advisory relationships with individual social scientists or with research centers.

THE REFORMULATION AND REFINEMENT OF THE COMMISSION MANDATE

From the outset, the mandate to the Commission was broad in scope. It was charged with investigating the amount and seriousness of crime in the United States and the effectiveness of the criminal justice system's response to it. It was also charged with exploring the underlying causes of crime and delinquency and the best means for prevention and control. The initial disposition of the Commission, the chairman, and most staff members was to interpret this mandate conservatively. It was not seen as desirable for the Commission to expend this opportunity and its resources on exploring a radical analysis of the crime problem in the United States or radical attempts to deal with it. Such an approach seemed unlikely to gain wide acceptance or to lead to any successful reform of the existing system. Accordingly, the major task forces were organized on traditional lines that tended to lend strength to conservative agency constituencies in each of the task force areas. This was, of course, less true in the Assessment Task Force and in a number of the sub-task forces devoted to special crime problems.

However, during the course of the Commission's work, a progressive liberalization of this conservative initial formulation gradually took place. This came about from the necessity to confront the facts of crime and the relative ineffectiveness of the criminal justice system; from trying to develop adequate explanations for these failures; and from the pressure to arrive at recommendations that were new and substantially significant to the operation of the criminal justice system in the prevention and control of crime.

In reflecting on the work of the Commission, I do not feel that the Commission was faced at the outset with the necessity to document or recommend any specific predetermined policy. The basic obligation was simply to find how to make the existing system work better, which, as I have already noted, rested on conservative premises committed to gradual reform. Unquestionably, individual members of the Commission and staff held preconceived positions on various policy issues and their resolution. These undoubtedly became incorporated into the final report of the Commission as work proceeded. But they faced the test of competing points of view and new evidence generated in the Commission's work. As the Commission's work proceeded, and conflicting points of view with regard to public policy in the area of criminal justice began to be identified among members of the Commission and staff, certain other latent constraints began to become manifest.

From the beginning, the chairman, the executive director, and most Commission members attached great importance to arriving at a consensus report without the need to present minority views. The process of communication among Commission and staff members was designed to forestall the development of sharply conflicting positions and to achieve a compromise position wherever possible. The chairman showed considerable ingenuity and talent in his capacity to search out and negotiate compromise positions when serious conflicts developed.[5] He was greatly assisted in this at both the Commission and staff levels by the executive and deputy directors of the Commission.

---

[5]It was of some significance to the later implementation of the Commission's report that Katzenbach was asked by the President to give up his position as Attorney General and become Under-Secretary of State. This event occurred during one of the Commission meetings. Katzenbach acceded to this request, but retained his chairmanship of the Crime Commission. His successor as Attorney General, Ramsey Clark, attended meetings but was never fully integrated in the work of the Commission, which by the fall of 1966, was nearing completion. There was a general feeling among staff and a few Commission members that this change in the chairman's federal role diminished the chances for vigorous pursuit and implementation of the Commission objectives at the federal level, despite Ramsey Clark's concurrence in many of these recommendations. They were not a product of his effort and involvement to the same degree.

A further constraint lay in the desire to produce a report that had maximum possibility of implementation at state and local levels. In some cases this led to the decision to suppress or subordinate highly charged emotional issues, such as capital punishment, marijuana use, or wiretapping. It was repeatedly stressed that the entire work of the Commission would be lost if public attention at the time of publication of the report were focused on these emotional issues, with the conflicting positions being expressed. Although all such loaded issues were discussed sometimes at great length and with great conviction, they were seen as basically unresolvable within the mandate of the Commission, and they were passed on for further discussion and ultimate resolution by other groups, such as Congress or state and local governments.

The imposition of such constraints served to keep conflict to a minimum, while preserving a climate wherein the liberal sentiments of the staff and certain Commission members could find maximum expression in the final recommendations. One device by which this was accomplished was through the creation of sub-task forces. For example, the creation of a sub-task force on juvenile delinquency provided the best form within which to deal with broad issues of delinquency prevention. In the context of assessing the causes of delinquency, it proved possible to secure sweeping recommendations to reorganize the nation's priorities in dealing with racism, urban development, the structure of ghetto communities, education and family life, recreation and job training, and placement opportunities. Though these recommendations went far beyond incremental reform of the criminal justice system, and instead addressed basic inadequacies in the allocation of the resources of American society, such statements proved tolerable in the context of better treatment for underprivileged and disadvantaged children.

By way of contrast, the issue of decriminalizing different types of offenses in the area of victimless crimes seemed too difficult a package to deal with in one place. Accordingly, the problems of drunkenness and narcotics abuse were withdrawn and addressed by separate sub-task forces. There were also special concerns of the Commission which cut across task force lines. A problem of this kind might be handled more successfully in a sub-task force devoted to it alone. For example, organized crime could not be adequately addressed if its subject areas were divided among the four major task forces. It seemed likely that emerging recommendations would carry more weight if the assessment of the organized crime problem and police, prosecution, and court enforcement practices were dealt with as a unit. This approach was also valid in trying, for the first time, to bring significant resources from science and technology to bear on the operation of the criminal justice system. Thus, as the work of the Commission progressed, reformulation and refinement of its mandate took place continually.

To offer a final example of mandate-shaping, several members of the staff were strongly in favor of having a sub-task force consider the problem of white-collar crime. This seemed a desirable means of communicating an awareness by the Commission that "crime in the streets" is not the whole crime problem of America, nor even its most costly, in terms of both lives and property. There was, however, little tolerance for this viewpoint among Commission members and a number of the staff. The expenditure of significant attention to white-collar crime seemed to depart too far from the Commission mandate; that is, to address the roots of "crime in the streets." Accordingly, the subject of white-collar crime was reduced to a chapter in the task force volume of Assessment of the Crime Problem.

THE COMMISSION'S RECOMMENDATIONS

Task force staff members played the primary role in developing recommendations, but they made considerable use of advisors and consultants and were sensitive to several issues about which Commission members had strong feelings. For example, the Commission was strongly divided on such issues as the treatment of marijuana or narcotic drug users, the desirability of wiretapping legislation to strengthen intelligence and enforcement capabilities in the organized crime area, capital punishment, or the effect of liberal Supreme Court decisions (e.g., *Escobedo, Miranda*) as a handicap to law enforcement. In such instances, the polarization of the Commission and also of the staff made it impossible to resolve the issues into clearly defined action recommendations. The common result was to defer resolution and to urge further study by legislative bodies at the federal, state, or local level.

During the first few months of the Commission's work, the staffs of the task forces were urged by the executive director to anticipate the recommendations that would likely flow from the research and consulting activities just getting underway. Thus, early in the process, task force staffs focused attention repeatedly on the final product, developed tentative recommendations, and tried to outline the types of supporting data that would be required to make them tenable. By the end of the summer of 1966, two-thirds of the way through the Commission's work, the task forces were required to produce tentative drafts of recommendations and supporting data. These were discussed with the technical advisory panels of the task forces and also with the Commission members assigned to work with each of the task forces. The task forces were then required to produce drafts for approval by the full Commission to be included in the final general report of the Commission.

While this process of forming recommendations were going on during the summer of 1966, consultant papers and research information gradually began to come in. These results often arrived so late in the work of the Commission that they were useful merely to provide supporting data for decisions already taken or as additional justification for such decisions.

Social science concepts, theories, and general perspectives were probably of greater utility to the staff and the Commission in forming the final recommendations than were the inputs from new knowledge development efforts funded by the Commission as research projects. Advice from the technical advisory panel and other consultants together with staff surveys of the literature constituted the primary resource for staff in assessing the state of knowledge in the field. Theories that seemed to be supported by this current knowledge were then relied upon to suggest action implications. Thus, consultant papers, fact-finding by staff, and the results of research projects provided supportive data and persuasive arguments for recommendations and general strategies for crime control and prevention, which had already been tentatively formulated by drawing on expert social science and professional opinion. Existing social science theories and data were drawn upon to formulate broad general strategies in the prevention and control of crime. The staff then developed more detailed recommendations that would serve to implement these strategies through new public policies, allocation of public resources, and proposals for change in the specific operation and organization of criminal justice agencies.

The greatest strength of the social science contribution lay in providing sensitizing concepts and theories, which oriented the search for solutions of the crime problem along certain paths. For example, studies of the correctional system and the operation of law enforcement and the courts, which had been made by social scientists for some years prior to the work of the Commission, had raised grave doubts about the effectiveness of existing criminal justice policies or of rehabilitation and treatment efforts. Studies of the labeling and stigmatizing effects of processing by the criminal justice system together with the high rates of recidivism constituted a convincing body of theory and fact, which led to the conclusion that the criminal justice system should be used only as a last resort in the control of undesirable conduct. On the basis of such knowledge and persuasive speculation, the Commission adopted the view that persons should be diverted from the criminal justice system into alternative systems of social control wherever possible. It recommended careful consideration of the possibility of decriminalizing certain offenses against morals or public order. It called for a reconsideration of the whole area of consensual crimes, or "crimes without victims," and questioned the appropriateness of status offenses for children that were not criminal offenses for adults. The documentation by sociologists of the corrosive effects of prison subcultures encouraged a broad policy of deprisonization of the criminal justice system and the development of a diverse range of community-based treatment alternatives.

The most important inputs of social science knowledge to the Crime Commission were probably (1) the documentation of the harmful consequences of existing practices and policies and (2) the suggestion of a variety of persuasive theories and justifications for pursuing alternative courses. The utility of social science facts and theories was not to suggest specific actions or programs, but rather broad general strategies for public policy and for reorganizing criminal justice agencies. As these general strategies emerged during the early months of the Commission's work, through interaction among the staff, Commissioners, and consultants; the major outline of the Commission's report took shape. Thereafter, the staff worked at a furious pace to develop arguments and data, to integrate consultant reports and research findings, and to use these to deal with inconsistencies and alternative proposals.

As the foregoing comments indicate, there were many problems in developing an effective input of social science theory, concepts, and research knowledge. The relevant social science literature was descriptive and analytical. There were relatively few experimental or controlled studies of the effectiveness of particular programs or policies. Explanations concerning the sources of crime and the functioning of the criminal justice system, though informative, lacked specific action implications. In addition, the sociologists serving as consultants to the Commission were reluctant to specify the logical implications of their analyses in the form of action recommendations for the Commission. When they did try to do this, the recommendations were often more influenced by personal ideological conviction than by appropriately organized facts and theories as arguments.

One of the most difficult problems was the slow pace of research sponsored by the Commission—so out of phase with the inexorable timetable of writing deadlines, Commission meetings, and approval procedures for recommendations. Most recommendations had to be drawn in anticipation of research findings, rather than from final reported results.

This discrepancy in the phasing of research and task force report requirements facilitated (among staff, Commission members, and consultants) an informal process of clique formation around ideologically favored positions on general policies and strategies. I have encountered a conspiratorial explanation of how Commissions are formulated and their activities directed toward certain predetermined ends. My own experiences and observations of the Crime Commission were quite different. Many of the participants held strong views about particular problems of crime and criminal justice and how they should be dealt with. However, no one that I knew held a clearly formulated agenda of either problems or recommendations for the Commission in its early days. Instead, there emerged informal groupings of persons who shared similar, but nonspecific, ideological views about the causes of crime and delinquency and the effectiveness of existing criminal justice policies. For example, there were those who saw criminal offenders as essentially exploited underdogs of a repressive social system, especially offenders from minority groups in large urban areas and the rural South. This faction in the staff and the Commission advocated the plight of the poor and the discriminated-against urban classes who needed something more than greater repression by law enforcement agencies to deal with the problems that led to their acts of violence and crimes against persons and property. Another faction stressed variations of a law-and-order approach. It was critical of permissive trends in the society and felt that restraints on individual misconduct needed to be reinforced by strong laws and punitive measures by criminal justice agencies. There also developed a small group of Commission members and staff who shared grave concern about the growth of organized crime, its capacity for subverting the normal processes of legitimate business and governance, and the inability of law enforcement agencies to contain it.

As these factional groups emerged and gained identity in the process of developing Commission recommendations, the executive director and chairman of the Commission were hard pressed to avoid ideological confrontations that would polarize and fractionate the Commission report and staff effort. They maintained constant pressure to keep the recommendations closely tied to factually supported premises or to theoretical views that could be shared in common. At the same time, these informal ideological factions generated strong motivation to produce persuasive factual and theoretical support for the arguments and recommendations proposed to the full Commission. The problem such divisions might create for the Commission's work was clearly recognized by the chairman and the executive director, and the divisions were firmly kept under control. Wherever possible, the divergent positions were elicited in advance of Commission meetings, and compromise proposals were worked out where that seemed necessary.

An important structural aid in this process proved to be the device of assigning Commission members to particular task force and sub-task force groups. These Commission members became articulate spokesmen and advocates for their task force recommendations before the full Commission. Other Commission members, unable to dig as deeply into the background data and theories on which these recommendations rested, were inclined to defer to those Commission members who had done so. Task force staff were therefore encouraged to involve sympathetic Commission members in their work, especially those likely to be most persuasive as advocates of their recommendations. As a consequence, this process led to far more liberal recommendations by the Commission than one would have thought possible at the outset, given the conservative cast of its membership. For many Commission and staff members, the task force work was a general learning experience, bringing together issues, facts, and theories in a systematic way to address problems which they had not been forced to consider in such depth before. Many of them became advocates of policies that they might not have thought feasible at the beginning. The development of task force reports and recommendations is an intensely consuming process of putting facts, ideas, general policies, and theories together in ways which most of the participants had not been required to do before. In some cases, this involvement of Commission members with task force staff and personnel led to sharp ideological confrontations for which no immediate resolution could be found. One such issue, for example, developed around recommendations with regard to the legalization of marijuana use.

IMPACT AND IMPLEMENTATION OF THE COMMISSION'S WORK

Early in its work the commission became concerned with the possibilities for implementation of its final recommendations. The chairman, executive director of the Commission, and many staff members were acutely conscious of the fact that a Presidential Commission has no enduring life and must rely on other established institutions and agencies to implement the results of its work. Considerable concern was expressed that the ultimate delivery of new crime control and prevention measures had to take place at state and local levels. Unless the Presidential Commission could involve states and localities in the concerns of the Commission and prepare them to continue the work of the Commission, not much could be accomplished in the long run.

Accordingly, a strategy was developed to award grants of $25,000 for staffing state planning committees. Such committees would assemble facts and interested persons in each state to review their crime and delinquency problems and consider the relevance of the Commission's recommendation for local application. Slightly more than half of the states responded and developed such state planning agencies. Representatives from these agencies and from other states attended a conference in Washington in October 1966, at which the President spoke.

Other implementation steps were also taken. Funds were set aside for a massive mailing of the Crime Commission's reports throughout the country. Copies were sent to all members of Congress and state legislatures and also to police, correctional agencies, and courts throughout the country. They were also sent to members of professional and academic groups concerned with problems of crime or criminal justice. For example, copies of the reports were mailed to all members of the Criminology Section of the American Sociological Association.

During the final months of the Commission's work, staff members participated in the development of new legislation, which would implement the recommendations of the Commission at the federal level, and provide the resources needed to support new state and local enterprises. This bill was introduced in 1967, but it did not receive final approval until 1968. Popularly known as the Safe Streets Act of 1968, one of its major accomplishments was to create a new agency in the Department of Justice, called the Law Enforcement Assistance Administration (LEAA). The funds allocated to this agency have steadily increased, and the budget was $880 million for fiscal year 1975.

LEAA is charged with the responsibility of providing technical assistance and information to the states and local communities, to distribute block grants to the states for law enforcement purposes based on a population formula, to provide discretionary grants for research and demonstration, and to promote training of criminal justice personnel. Within LEAA is the National Institute of Law Enforcement and Administration of Justice, which undertakes research and demonstration projects of its own as well as financing those initiated by others. The National Institute is also charged with the responsibility of developing an information clearinghouse and statistics on crime and delinquency. One direct result of the Commission's work in this area is a contract between the National Institute and the Bureau of the Census to conduct large-scale surveys of the victims of crime so that trend data of this type might be developed to supplement reporting by police agencies.

The state planning agencies stimulated by the Commission have now been established in all states and constitute the conduit and planning agency for the distribution of block grants from LEAA. The executive director of the Commission, James Vorenberg, in a May, 1972 article in *Atlantic* magazine, reviewed the developments of the five years following the submission of the Commission report. His review expresses considerable disappointment with the excessive law-and-order preoccupations of policies and funding decisions within LEAA. He maintains that the current national administration and the state and local planning agencies have been most conservative in utilizing the new funds, and have made little progress in implementing the more than 200 recommendations that the National Crime Commission set forth.

It is important to note, however, that a whole new structure at federal, state and local levels now exists for channeling money directly to improvements in the criminal justice system and to programs of crime prevention and control. Throughout the states new competence is developing to plan and implement programs of an experimental character. Moreover, these programs are being required to justify themselves by undertaking detailed evaluations of the impact of their work. It should also be noted that a number of Presidential Commissions that followed the Crime Commission picked up and reinforced many of the themes, recommendations, and general strategies proposed by the Crime Commission. The impact of the Crime Commission has been made much greater because of the work of these other Commissions. They provided important endorsement and validation of many of the recommendations reached by the Crime Commission while dealing with violence, campus unrest and other problems.

Unquestionably, the change of administration in 1968 disrupted the logical development of the Crime Commission's work. The new administration, under President Nixon, adopted a strong law-and-order approach to the crime problem and, in fact, established the new National Advisory Commission on Criminal Justice Standards and Goals to give greater expression to this ideological commitment than appeared in the report of the Katzenbach Crime Commission.

CONCLUSION

It is clear that the National Crime Commission report could not have been written without the help of sociologists and social science knowledge. The input was an important one in innumerable ways. During the Commission's tenure, the pressure to produce the report gave little time for original research. The Commission had to exploit existing knowledge and to draw recommendations from the existing state of theory and fact in the field. Sociologists were extensively consulted to draw on their knowledge of crime problems and of criminal justice agencies. Often, however, the results were disappointing. The launching of the Commission early in the academic year made it difficult to recruit staff. Consultants invariably were busy with academic and research work of their own and could find little time to give serious attention to preparing careful reports for the Commission's work. There were, of course, many valuable and important exceptions. However, more often than not, consultants produced hasty reports that failed to identify issues clearly or failed to organize facts and theories in response to them. Almost invariably, there was a great reluctance to make policy recommendations. Most of the reports represented summaries of the literature and occasionally, ideological polemics. In other reports, analysis proceeded at too high a level of abstraction. Some of the research work for the Commission charted new paths in developing data useful for policy purposes. But the pressure of deadlines sometimes prevented careful work, which resulted in sketchy reports of progress rather than in final results.

The Presidential Commission has serious limitations as a vehicle for promoting important research of the problems it is called on to address. Its composition and mandate frequently prevent it from exploring or advocating radically new approaches to problems. It can, however, do a credible job of pulling together existing knowledge in the field, tracing out theoretical and factual implications for action, and it does command a wide audience for the assimilation of its findings. Sociologists have much to contribute in this forum for the development of public policy. The survey technique for research is especially well suited to a rapid assessment of the dimensions of a problem and public attitudes and reactions to it. The work of the National Crime Commission demonstrated that sociologists have much to contribute. They can become even more constructive in their contributions as they learn to organize their knowledge and theory so as to facilitate the choice of alternative policy recommendations.

PART TWO

DISCUSSION

CHAPTER FIVE

The Uses of Sociology
by Presidential Commissions

PAUL F. LAZARSFELD AND MARTIN JAECKEL
Department of Sociology, University of Pittsburgh

INTRODUCTION

In 1962 the senior author proposed to the Executive Committee of the American Sociological Association that a central theme for the convention be the uses of sociology. The plan did not work well: most of the speakers did not comply. Instead of talking about the uses of sociology by various institutions—say, the courts or hospitals or business corporations—the speakers thought of the whole session as a continuation of the convention that had resulted in a very successful American Sociological Association publication, *Sociology Today*; and the papers updated the sociology of law, of medicine, of business. The reason for the miscarriage was twofold: the contributors were not much interested in the problem of application and little factual knowledge was available even if a speaker had been willing to conform. As a consequence, it was decided to try a replay, a kind of shadow convention that would better reflect the original intention. The Executive Council appointed an editorial committee, consisting of Sewell, Wilensky, and Lazarsfeld, who invited a new group of sociologists

117

to contribute to the volume. The result, after several years of effort, was *The Uses of Sociology* (New York: Basic Books, 1967). The volume did not have the coherence we had hoped for, but many of the contributions reflected the basic idea, an effort to make the utilization of sociology a topic of systematic research in its own right. A forty-page introduction by the editors mapped out the elements of such a program. At the conclusion of this introduction, the editors described what the next step should be:

> One can understand with hindsight, but it comes as a surprise, how difficult it is to find out how and where sociology is being used. The Loomises report that they wrote to several hundred rural sociologists about the uses of sociology; only those who were actively connected with some administrative enterprise could give concrete examples. In connection with O. M. Hyman's paper, a questionnaire was sent to the members of the A.S.A. section on medical sociology; the majority of the respondents had only vague ideas of what happened to their own work. Clients seem to be more likely to know of uses than the sociologists themselves. But not only are clients difficult to sample; they are often corporations, in which the officers who may have acted on the basis of a report are not easily traced. A future theory of uses will require experimentation with various ways of gathering information.

We have taken this advice seriously. At Columbia University as well as at the University of Pittsburgh, funds were obtained to collect descriptive material on a large number of concrete situations where sociological studies or ideas were applied. One of the sources that seemed fruitful to us were Presidential Commissions: the roles of sociological expertise and social research in their work.

The senior author held a general seminar on the topic while still at Columbia. Several Commissions seem to be well documented, but one offered a special opportunity for a more detailed inquiry. The Social Research Director of the Kerner Commission on Riots, Robert Shellow, is now on the faculty of Carnegie-Mellon University in Pittsburgh. He was willing to share with the junior author of this essay his files and his experiences, which then were supplemented by inspection of the material deposited in the National Archives. We were thus well prepared when the

Association President Komarovsky organized the plenary Presidential Commissions. We had available the general scheme of work developed at Columbia and the detailed case study worked upon at Pittsburgh.

The participants in the meeting, who are also the contributors to the present volume, sent us in advance the essays they prepared on the commissions in which each of them played a major role. On the basis of these papers the senior author addressed the convention: this chapter is an extension of these comments, and is divided into three parts. The Columbia project, supported by a grant from the Office of Naval Research, distinguished between the cognitive and organizational aspects of commission analysis. We are concentrating here on the cognitive aspect, what we call the process of utilization. The first part of the chapter reproduces this "cognitive map" and examplifies it from the experiences reported by the four main participants.

The next two parts elaborate two remarks by the first discussant, Raymond Mack. One of his suggestions was that the American Sociological Association might appoint a committee after each Presidential Commission that would study the role sociologists and sociology played within each commission. We applaud this idea, but we wanted to stress how much work is involved in such a plan. The junior author has spent more than a year analyzing just one commission. In part two, we report just one piece of his work because it is likely to have general importance: the partial comparison between the official published report of the Kerner Commission and some of the unpublished material made available by Dr. Shellow.

The final part combines a suggestion by Mack and remarks that pervade all the contributions. Why is it that sociologists play such a small role in Presidential Commissions and are easily subdued by lawyers? One reason certainly is that graduate training in sociology does not adequately prepare the student for future work in Presidential Commissions and similar agencies. To meet this need, the Sociology Department at the University of Pittsburgh has begun to develop a special program in applied sociology, with the initial support of an NSF grant. The program requires practical work in addition either to course work for the MA or the PHD degree in sociology. In part three we report the plans and first experiences of this program.

PART ONE: THE PROCESS OF UTILIZATION

It seems helpful to divide the process of utilization into a number of phases. Not all of them occur in all situations and each phase has consequences for the subsequent ones. Very often the whole cycle has to be gone through more than once. The papers of the four main contributors provide valuable illustrations. We, therefore, just list the seven phases, illustrated by a graph. The examples taken from the four commissions will clarify what we have in mind:

- *Step 1:* Formulation of problem.
- *Step 2:* Setting up the necessary staff.
- *Step 3:* Translating the practical problem into a design of inquiry.
- *Step 4:* Organizing the available and acquired knowledge.
- *Step 5:* The road to recommendations.
- *Step 6:* The implementation of the plan of action.
- *Step 7:* Assessment and possible reentry of the cycle.

MAP OF UTILIZATION

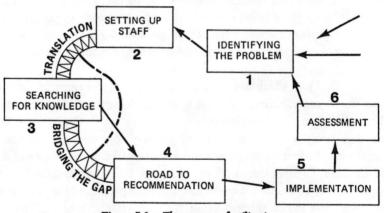

Figure 5-1. The process of utilization.

Step One: Origin and identification of the problem

The four Commissions show considerable variation in the nature of their origins and of the mandates that resulted.

In the case of the Crime Commission, the general problem of violence had already been a political issue for several years, ever since the assassination of President Kennedy in 1963. Senator Goldwater had made "crime in the streets" a theme of his 1964 campaign. And there was an interest on President Johnson's part in preventing the urban confrontations that were developing out of the Great Society programs from becoming a similar issue in the elections of 1968. A Presidential Commission seemed an appropriate vehicle for launching a federal initiative concerning "crime in the streets," without unduly encroaching on state and local law enforcement responsibilities.

As it turned out, the largely nonfederal law enforcement and criminal justice systems constituted the main objects of the Commission's investigations. Apart from the assessment of the crime problem and the suggestion of general remedies, the mandate called for a review of these systems and for recommendations for administrative reforms. The question it seems was how, and to what points, to channel the federal funds that were to be committed.

By way of contrast, the Eisenhower Commission, which had its more immediate crisis, focused more directly on the phenomenon of violence itself. Constituted in 1968 in the wake of the assassinations of Martin Luther King and of Robert Kennedy, the Commission was charged with investigating the general causes of lawless forms of violence, as well as their prevention.

Both the Commissions on Pornography and on population Growth were created by Acts of Congress rather than by Executive Order. Perhaps this feature reflects the structure of the issues involved, that is, the long-range character of such issues, as well as the tentative status of government activities in these areas. In the case of the Pornography Commission, Congress had already been processing Commission proposals for five years. Those who wanted to suppress obscenity by legislation were ranged against so-called libertarians who objected to governmental regulation of such matters. President Johnson would, in fact, have preferred not to have to deal with the topic. The breakthrough came in 1967 when the study of "effects," that is, of exposure to pornographic materials, was included in the mandate. The one group assumed that "ill" or socially harmful effects would be demonstrated, whereas the other wanted to have the various conditioning relationships investigated before anything was decided. Thus, the same mandate served divergent sets of expectations.

In the case of the Population Commission, the plurality of interested parties is reflected in a plurality of practical perspectives with respect to which future population growth was to be studied. Ecologists' concerns were represented in the mandate to assess the implications of population growth for natural resources and for the quality of the environment; family planners' purposes in a mandate to investigate the means of achieving a suitable population level; and the administration's interest in the topic was to assess the implications of population growth and internal migration for the public sector of the national economy and for the activities of federal, state and local government, respectively.

Step Two: Building up the research staff

Given the original formulation of the general problem, there still remains the question of how to conduct the investigation. The machinery that is set up and the methods that are used amount to an operational definition of the appropriate approach. The choice of procedures is, in part, guided by the substantive themes that devolve from a Commission's interpretation of its mandate. The Commission on Population Growth, for example, chose to regard its mission as "interventionist" rather than "accommodationist." According to Westoff, it interpreted its basic charge as that of recommending a national population policy rather than developing a master plan to prepare for continued population increase.

But independent of the substantive choices that a Commission makes, there are certain general points of research strategy that must be settled as well. In setting up its staff, a Commission can choose between (1) having its own central staff do most of the investigative work, or (2) contracting it out in the form of separate studies, which option initially, at least, conserves time, energy, and funds.

The Population Commission followed the latter procedure, which necessitated considerable synthesizing efforts at the end of its work. In the other three Commissions, the Commission or its staff were organized into task forces and panels, according to the major aspects of the problem.

The choice of topics that a Commission assigns to its task forces constitutes a crucial step in the operational translation of its task. The Crime Commission, for example, focused largely on certain criminal justice constituencies in establishing task forces on the police, the courts, and the corrections system, respectively. The general societal problem of crime was addressed via a fourth force on the "assessment" of the crime problem. A fifth task force on "science and technology" was added later in an effort to incorporate the use of modern "systems" methodologies. And finally, a number of sub-task forces were organized to study special forms of crime: juvenile delinquency, organized crime, narcotics and drug abuse, and drunkenness offenses.

Conversely, Commissions may also decide not to devote task forces to certain topics. Short reports that the Violence Commission considered the suggestion to have a task force on war, but that idea was abandoned. Instead, war was included in the province of the task forces on "History and Comparative Perspectives" and "Demonstrations, Protests, and Group Violence." "The effect of this decision," Short points out, "was to focus attention on the war in Indochina as a source of social disruption rather than on the political responsibilities for war-making".

The assignment of individuals to task forces also makes a difference in the proceedings. Ohlin reports that in the Crime Commission, the assignment of Commission members to specialized task forces had a "liberalizing" effect on their views. Task force work turned out to be a general learning experience. It exposed them individually to issues, facts, and theories which they had generally not been forced to consider as closely before. Many of them subsequently became advocates, before the full Commission, of policies that they might originally have rejected out of hand.

The Violence Commission introduced the innovation of having joint task force directors, one a lawyer and one a social scientist. However, this form appears to have operated less efficiently than teams headed by one specialist. Incidentally, the Violence Commission's deliberate emphasis on research and the recruitment of social scientists led to another interesting consequence; namely, the decision to substitute a "neutral" definition of violence for the definition contained in the mandate, which focused on acts of lawlessness. When the time came for making recommendations, however, the Commission reverted to the latter, the "official" definition of violence.

Step Three: Translating the basic problem into a search for information

A Commission's search for information can be conducted in many ways, which may include field trips by Commissioners, hearings, surveys, and even regular experiments. In most cases, a variety of approaches and procedures are combined. Larsen has properly stressed the unique role of experiments in the Pornography Commission.

Another general issue is whether or not original research should be conducted. Prime considerations are available time as well as funds. In the case of the Campus Unrest Commission, which existed for only one summer, it was decided to let experts review the state of knowledge in the field. Conversely, in the case of the Violence Commission, original research was decided upon, because existing knowledge was judged to be altogether inadequate.

A further decision point is the question whether or not to have hearings. Researchers tend not to favor them, but lawyers and politicians do. James Short reports that he changed his opinion about the utility of hearings after experiencing them, and lists several purposes which they may serve:

> A) They provide a forum—even a dramatic forum—for staff to bring points of view to the Commission. Skolnick refers to communication through emotional engagement as the "ultimate art" of "social science as theater" B) The hearings were a quick way to confront the Commissioners with information and points of view before Task Forces were ready with systematic information and analysis. The Commission thus got an early start in deliberation. C) Most of the hearings were public, and they were well covered by the media. The Commission's activities thus received invaluable public attention to the problems they were studying.

Similar purposes, in particular, the intention to give interested organizations an opportunity to present their views, are reported for the Pornography and for the Population Commission.

The uses that the several Commissions made of national public opinion surveys illustrate well the broad and diverse purposes which a general research procedure can be made to serve. The Crime Commission initiated a national survey of criminal victimization to determine the extent of unreported crime, the attitudes of victims and citizens toward crime, and the measures they took to defend themselves. This survey constituted a major innovation in the study of crime and crime rates, because it penetrated beyond the information available in police reports. The Violence Commission also used a national survey to probe the public's experience with violence and the context of related attitudes; in particular, media preferences and usage, political beliefs and habits, and gun ownership.

The Pornography Commission commissioned a national probability sample survey to identify the extent of the public's exposure to erotic materials as well as the correlates of such exposure, and to ascertain the generally held normative views concerning restrictions on the consumption of erotica. (On the whole, the public's views turned out to be much more "permissive" than might have been anticipated.) The Population Commission, finally, conducted a national opinion poll to gauge the state of public information with respect to population topics and attitudes concerning the related matters of city size, immigration, abortion, and population planning. Ohlin believes that the survey technique for research helps not only to assess the dimensions of a problem, but also public attitudes and reactions to it.

Step Four: Organizing acquired knowledge

It is a truism that the usefulness of the information that a Commission acquires depends on the manner in which this knowledge is organized. One of the major determinants of this organization is the timetable that a Commission sets for itself. The Pornography Commission, for example, conducted what amounted to an open-ended search for information, and only at the end, considered what the implications would be for various policy options. Larsen points out that the strong commitment to research per se prevented due consideration of policy issues, which thereby weakened the impact that the Commission's studies might otherwise have had:

> I now see that we missed a rare opportunity to link social research to social policy in an effective manner. We failed because we did not turn our tools first to an empirical analysis of policy options so that the remainder of the research on effects, etc., would illuminate the costs and consequences of realistic alternative courses of action. In short, we did not have a policy-research theory to guide our strategy.

The other extreme, a high degree of organization, is exemplified by the Crime Commission. Early in the Commission's work, the task force staffs were forced to map out the possible lines of argument and thus to organize the search for supporting information.[1] Ohlin stated that:

> . . . the task force staff focused attention repeatedly on the final product, developed tentative recommendations, and tried to outline the types of supporting data that would be required to make them tenable. By the end of the summer of 1966, two-thirds of the way through the Commission's work, the task forces were required to produce tentative drafts of recommendations and supporting data.

The feature that we wish to emphasize is the concretely anticipatory character of the manner in which the Commission's work proceeded—a feature perhaps best exemplified by the preparations that the Commission undertook to secure the implementation of its recommendations.

The other two cases fall between the indicated extremes. The Violence Commission divided its work into roughly three six-month phases: first, a period of initial research and investigations, which culminated in a progress report to the President; second, the drafting of Commission statements on the various topics; and third, the serial release of separate task force statements, followed by the official Summary Report. The social science research staff (and the physical presence of the research directors) was diminished in the latter two phases, a condition that may have contributed to the Commission's regressing from the "neutral" definition of violence, which it had earlier accepted. The Population Commission also published an Interim Report, which described the importance of the general topic, the demographic situation, and the subjects being explored, but which presented little in the way of conclusions. The main controversies apparently only surfaced later.

The public impact of a Commission's findings partially depends on the manner in which they are presented. The Population Commission's report contains especially good examples. The Commission faced the task of presenting the demographic projections that underlie its analysis of the consequences of various forms of population growth as concisely as possible. At issue was the demonstration of the relationship between a set

---

[1]This type of procedure may be one of the reasons for the fact, noted by Ohlin, that social science concepts and perspectives probably contributed more to the forming of the final recommendations than did the inputs from the new knowledge development efforts funded by the Commission as research projects.

of fairly involved demographic projections (with respect to population size as well as to age distributions) and the economic, environmental, and fiscal consequences that were expected to follow. The device chosen was to graphically compare the consequences of the two-child versus the three-child family for resource and energy consumption and the like. This ingenuous simplification well conveys a sense of the range within which future developments are expected to fall.

Another example, which illustrates the organization of information for the purpose of persuasion, is given in the Commission's descriptions of alternative paths to population stabilization. The National Fertility Studies of 1965 and 1970 had yielded information on the incidence of unwanted births in the population. The Commission's declared interest in ways to stabilize population growth led to the demographic exercise of projecting population developments without this component. The resulting estimates revealed that the elimination of unwanted fertility would take the nation most of the way to stationary reproduction. It is difficult, Westoff points out, to overestimate the suggestiveness of this finding. "It meant that instead of trying to change a social norm, through politically difficult means, the Commission could concentrate instead on trying to provide the means to satisfy couples' apparent goals through the improvement and distribution of methods of fertility control, a 'solution' well within acceptable political limits." Similarly, the demonstration that if women averaged 2.0 rather than 2.1 births, zero population growth could be achieved in spite of continued immigration, was influential, Westoff reports, in defeating a recommendation to reduce the current volume of immigration.

Step Five: The road to recommendations

We cannot demonstrate the wealth of assumptions, constructs, and inventions that generally enter into the process of bridging the gap between knowledge that has been acquired and ultimate recommendations.

But a brief sketch of a few of the issues and controversies that arose in these Commissions will indicate the diversity in the assumptions that govern the use of such findings. The oscillation by the Violence Commission between a legitimacy-oriented and a "neutral" definition of violence has already been noted. Ohlin points out that for the Crime Commission, the creation of a sub-task force on juvenile delinquency made possible the discussion and inclusion in the report of "liberal" perspectives on general societal problems, which otherwise might not have been allowed to surface. In other words, societal reform topics that certain Commission members would not have accepted directly were deemed permissible in the context of securing conditions for the reform of disadvantaged youth.

A related phenomenon is the formation of ideological cliques of informal groupings of persons who share a broad outlook on the causes of the set of problems under discussion and on the relative effectiveness of various ameliorative policies. In the Crime Commission, for example, three factions emerged, representing concern about (1) criminal offenders as exploited underdogs, (2) a law-and-order approach, and (3) the growth of organized crime.

In the Population Commission, there were different basic perceptions of the population problem itself; namely, the "ecological" view, the "unwanted fertility" school, and the "social justice" perspective. Westoff points out that these ideological differences had more of an impact on the diagnosis of the population problem than on the final policy recommendations themselves. He stated: "This was not because the logic of the positions did not lead to different policy conclusions, but rather that everyone more or less recognized that any impact the Commission report might have would be seriously affected by the political and moral acceptability of the recommendations." The negotiated solution was to express the differences as "A Diversity of Views" in the Introduction to the Final Report and to concentrate on those policies that were consistent with all three positions.

In the case of the Pornography Commission, the main controversy revolved around the recommendation that legislation prohibiting the distribution of sexual materials to consenting adults should be repealed. Larsen reports that the Commission chairman shifted his position on this issue, on the basis of his assessment of the largely negative findings of the "effects" studies. "The evidence was overwhelming," Dean Lockhart is reported to have said, "that such materials do not contribute to antisocial behavior of any sort." Larsen goes on to extrapolate some analytical distinctions concerning the possible impact of such effects-studies, and the contribution of sociologists to such matters in general. He distinguishes three basic questions and corresponding degrees of competence on the part of sociologists. The first question concerns the *relative impact* of the factor under discussion (exposure to obscene materials) on the problem phenomenon (antisocial behavior); that is, the impact relative to the effects of other determinants. Sociologists are perhaps best equipped to contribute to the question of the determination of effects. The second question concerns the *degree of disutility* of the determined effects. Larsen points out that empirical evidence does not provide the criterion for this dimension, but that sociologists can, through opinion research, determine what people's general preferences are.

The third question is: *What level of intervention* is justified? Do the number of rapes that censorship permits us to avoid justify limitations on freedom of speech? Does the decrease in auto accidents made possible by Prohibition justify removing alcohol from everyone? This, Larsen says, is the primary policy question, and sociologists are no more qualified to answer it than are others, but what they can do is to clarify the options.

In the case of the Violence Commission's Task Force on Firearms, the determination of an "effects" relationship between the availability of guns (private gun ownership) and their use in violence led to the recommendation to restrict the former. A number of comparisons between cities and regions served to establish the relationship in questions. The most convincing evidence came from Detroit. Post-1967 increases in sales of handguns in that city were matched by marked increases in the rates of firearm accidents, of (the proportion of) firearms suicides, and of violent crimes committed with firearms (attacks, robberies, and homicides). Furthermore, it was established for the United States as a whole that firearms assaults are about five times as deadly as attacks with a knife, and that handguns account for three-fourths of all gun homicides (92 percent in large cities). This information is directly reflected in the Commission's recommendation that "concealable handguns, a common weapon used in violent crimes, must be brought under a system of restrictive licensing." Apparently the disutility of the deaths involved constituted the overriding consideration.

Step Six: Implementation of recommendations

Presidential Commissions, as temporary advisory bodies, are neither directly responsible for the implementation of their recommendations, nor for the further processing of the reports they have generated, once they themselves pass out of existence. This crucial phase of the utilization cycle must be left to their sponsors and to the public. But their efforts in producing the report are also geared to its reception. Anticipations of the impact and the repercussions of various formulations are known to enter into, perhaps even to govern, a Commission's final deliberations, and especially the stance of those Commissioners who represent special constituencies. Generally, the fiscal and political feasibility of recommended policies are presumed to be a major consideration in their formulation.

Our sample of cases yields some examples of concrete actions that were taken to prepare for or to monitor the developments in the post-Commission phase. The Population Commission, for example, divided the publication of its report into three sections—on the diagnosis of the problem, recommendations concerning reproduction, and recommendations concerning administrative measures, respectively—in order to prevent the resulting publicity from focusing exclusively on the abortion issues. It also planned to produce a video version of the report, for dissemination via the commercial television networks. This plan failed when the Commission insisted on complete editorial autonomy. A film was later made by an independent producer and was shown on national public television instead.

The prime example of preparation for the implementation of recommendations are the activities of the Crime Commission. The Commission was aware of the fact that the major part of its recommendations would have to be implemented at the level of state and local governments. Since the ultimate delivery of new crime control and prevention measures would have to take place at these levels, the executive staff decided to involve the states and localities in the concerns of the Commission and to prepare them to continue its work. It developed a strategy of awarding grants of $25,000 for the staffing of state planning committees, to assemble both the facts and interested persons to review their crime and delinquency problems in each state and to consider the relevance of the Commission's recommendations for local application. In October of 1966, several months before it went out of existence, the Commission sponsored a conference, which representatives from these and other state bodies attended, to stimulate plans for the reform of state criminal systems. Funds were set aside for a massive mailing of the Commission's reports to all members of Congress and of state legislatures, and also to police departments, correctional agencies, and courts throughout the country, as well as to members of related professional and academic groups. And finally, during the last months of the Commission's work, Ohlin said that "staff members participated in the development of new legislation which would implement at the federal level the recommendations of the commission and provide the resources needed to support new state and local enterprises in this area." This bill, popularly known as the Safe Streets Act of 1968, created a new agency (LEAA) in the Department of Justice, which is charged with funding and monitoring improvements and innovations in law enforcement and criminal justice programs, and also related demonstrations and research. Apart from the fact that political support already existed for these measures, the Crime Commission's success in fostering implementations derives from two sets of preparations:

1 The deliberate involvement of the prospective implementors in the planning of implementations.
2 The creation of agencies to monitor their development.

Perhaps these procedural steps deserve the attention and even the emulation of other groups of researchers in applied situations.

Step Seven: Assessment

Since there are no bodies directly charged with evaluating a Presidential Commission's findings, its recommendations, and their implementation, this phase of the utilization process remains rather diffuse. There are, of course, responses (including criticism or neglect) on the part of the sponsors (the President or Congress) and of interested constituencies. In the case of the Population Commission, the President's response focused on the issues of abortion and of contraceptive services for minors, reiterated his personal opposition to making either available, and, according to Westoff, disregarded "the (Commission's) basic analysis of the costs and benefits of population growth and the conclusion that population stabilization was desirable."

Sometimes the response takes the form of establishing yet another Commission, in the hope of obtaining competing, if not the desired, results. This occurred with respect to the Crime Commission in the Nixon administration's establishment of the National Commission on Criminal Justice Standards and Goals, which was supposed to emphasize a law-and-order approach, but which also began to develop liberalizing tendencies.

Sometimes deliberate efforts are made to review the impact of Presidential Commissions' reports. In 1968 the Joint Economic Committee of Congress, for example, conducted hearings on this topic. Two of the commissioners joined forces with the National Urban League to assess the "State of the Cities" three years after the Kerner Report. Finally, there is a form of evaluation which consists of the codified judgments of courts as to the positions that are to prevail. Three years after the Pornography Commission's report, the Supreme Court ruled that for the purpose of developing restrictive legislation, "effects" of obscene materials can be assumed and need not be proved by scientific inquiry, a decision which, by implication, declares much of the Commission's investigations to have been irrelevant for practical decision-making purposes. It remains to be seen whether this approach to the question remains tenable.

PART II: COMMISSION'S REPORT IN TWO GUISES: THE ROLE OF POLITICS

In Pittsburgh we are currently engaged in a study of the Kerner Commission and its report on the riots of 1967. With the help of Robert Shellow, the Commission's director for research, we are reviewing the role played by social science efforts in the work of the Commission. Its basic source of information on the riots was a set of field studies conducted in twenty-three of the cities that had experienced disorders. A general analysis of these field studies made by Shellow's team of social scientists in an internal report was suppressed, and a substitute effort by the investigative operations department was incorporated into the Commission's official report. We have selected the comparison between these two documents as an example of the type of work involved in tracing social science participation in a Presidential Commission.

The differences between the social scientists' analysis of the riots and the summary description that was finally adopted by the Commission are rather striking. The Shellow report carried the suggestive title: "The Harvest of American Racism—The Political Meaning of Violence in the Summer of 1967." The authors applied a broad social movement perspective and took a longitudinal approach to the topic. They concluded that an ever-increasing politicalization was the central trend in the ghettos as well as in the disorders. Ghetto youth were identified as a potent new social force, blocked from access to political power, and therefore tending toward some form of rebellion. At the same time, to expand their analysis of the disorders, the authors developed and used certain broad concepts (e.g., the difference between political confrontations and purely expressive rampages, the degree of political content in a disorder, and net assessments of the overall racial attitude of a city's elite). Finally, they extrapolated from their analysis the requirement that ghetto youth would have to be incorporated into local urban power systems (e.g., by giving them an expanded role in the design and organization of antipoverty programs), if further bloodshed were to be averted.

The summary produced by members of the executive staff and of the operations department contains none of the above systematizations. Instead, it presents an accurate composite description, an overall profile of the riots as factual events. The bulk of this overview consists of the enumeration of various component elements of the disorders—physical conditions, kinds of violence, types·and extents of damage, characteristics of participants, types of control action, demographic information on the areas in question, postriot reactions—with examples and frequencies of occurrence given for each item or category. The net result is a cross-sectional array of unrelated ingredients, from which little can be concluded. A number of substantive generalizations are, however, stated in the introduction. It is pointed out that riots develop out of a cumulative build-up of grievances and tensions. And the distressing social and economic conditions of life in the ghetto are presented as the underlying causes. The emphasis on socioeconomic rather than on political conditions was, in part, guided by a concern with those kind of improvements that federal administrative agencies could directly sponsor or undertake.

A few examples illustrate the divergence between the two summary reports, as well as the different ways in which the same pieces of information can be handled and incorporated into conflicting general interpretations. An obvious fact is that of riot violence. In the Harvest Report, the escalation of the riots is represented due to the confrontation between ghetto activists and the police, as revolving around political demands, as involving protests over the legitimacy of certain official use of force, and in the extreme, as resulting in outright competition for control over a certain territory. In the Commission's official report, the outbreak of violence and its further progress are described in the terminology of natural events, as a catastrophe that befalls a city as a result of the accumulation (and then precipitation) of certain tensions up to, and then beyond, an imaginary breaking point. The finding that, in most of the disorders, violence alternated with negotiations between rioters and city officials was used in the Harvest analysis to elaborate the category of a political disorder: in the official report, the fact of alternation is simply recorded as a remarkable phenomenon, and documented in fifty pages of seismographic charts on levels of violence and of law enforcement mobilization. The crucial finding that (male) ghetto youth were in the forefront of the disorders (with respect both to their numbers and their actions) is treated similarly. The Harvest Report views such riot participation as one form of a new political activism, as energies that can be expected to enter into the regular political process, if given the chance. The Commission's report again merely records the finding concerning age of the typical riot participant as a fact. Finally, there is the issue of ghetto community support for the rioters. The fact that active riot participants were a minority of the ghetto area population can be handled in several ways. The estimates of the proportion of active participants can be downgraded toward relative insignificance (as was done in the McCone report on the 1965 Los Angeles riot); the inactive majority can be assumed to have been silent supporters at least of the rioters' intentions, if not of their actions (which is the position taken in the Harvest Report); and finally, the finding (and therewith the issue) can be passed over completely (which is what occurred in the Commission's official report).

There are, of course, assessments of the riots on which the two reports agree. Both reports state that the 1967 riots were not race riots. Violence was not directed at white persons per se, but at white-owned property and at the representative of white authority. The reports also note the absence of a general conspiracy behind the rapid and often contiguous spread of the disorders. But even when both overviews concur in a general observation (e. g., the judgment that there was considerable variety in the disorders), they differ in its further elaboration. Given the fact of variety in the disorders, the Commission's report concludes that little can be said about the riot process in general, other than that it is unpredictable.

> We have been unable to identify constant patterns in all aspects of civil disorders. We have found that they are unusual, irregular, complex and, in the present state of knowledge, unpredictable social processes. Like many human events, they do not unfold in orderly sequences.

Faced with the same variety in the initial observations, the Harvest analysis attempts to determine several distinct principles, the operation of which singly or in combination will account for the patterns actually observed. The authors note that a broad range of events have come to be classified as riots. The term *riot* is used to refer to window-breaking by drunks as well as to a general social upheaval. It may refer to retaliatory violence by the police as well as by militant youth. The activities and intentions of the participants vary between disorders and even between phases of the same riot; they can be politically purposeful or merely opportunistic. The disorder can be anticipated, or ritually staged, more than it is real. The authors hence conclude:

> From these initial observations it becomes quite clear that the task of defining a riot is as thorny a problem as determining its causes. The dynamics of the various disorders we have studied indicate a variety of governing principles at work. The way these combine provide us with a broad picture of the various patterns of disorders that occurred in different cities.

Again, the fact that the postriot situations in the various cities present a mixed picture (on both the local and the general level) is taken, in the Commission's report, to imply that little basic change took place in the conditions underlying the disorders. The Harvest Report, on the other hand, presents the simultaneity of ameliorative efforts and of polarization between the races as a quickening of the general issue.

The characterizations of the two reports set out above are themselves reconstructions that are based on a variety of observations. It is, however, one thing to intuit differences in the governing conceptions, and another to document them. We have carried out a content analysis of the two summaries. Our comparisons are focused on the space allotted to various themes; on the kinds of specific materials included or not included in the review; on the devices used in presenting the material (headings and subheadings, charts, tables, prepositioned summaries); on the format of recommendations; and on the terminology in which the various observations are expressed. We shall conclude this section with a few examples to indicate the type and the amount of work involved in tracing substantive features of the kind sketched above.

Our examples are given in the form of general assertions about the two overviews, followed by some of the evidence that supports these generalizations. (The bases for the frequency counts that follow are Chapters 1–3 of the Harvest Report and the corresponding sections (namely, 1, 2, and 4) in Chapter 2 of the Commission's Report on the "Patterns of Disorder.")

I   Substantively, the Harvest Report has a political focus; that is, it concentrates on the political meaning of the riots, whereas the Kerner Commission's official Report focuses on socioeconomic conditions in the ghetto as the preconditions for disorders.

   1   The ratios in the use of the word "political" versus the use of some part of the phrase "severely disadvantaged social and economic conditions" are 95:0 for the Harvest Report, and 11:30 for the Kerner Commission's report, respectively.

   2   The ratios in the use of the words "protest" or "demands" versus the use of the words "grievances" or "complaints" are 35:21 for the Harvest Report, and 4:85 for the Kerner Commission's Report, respectively.

II The Harvest Report discusses the dynamics of confrontation between the rioters and the police; the Kerner Commission's Report uses the imagery of natural events.

   1   The Harvest Report uses the word "escalation" seven times, "competition" eight times, "aggressive" (rioters) eight times, and "confrontation" eighteen times. None of these expressions occur in the Kerner Commission's description, except for "confrontation," two times.

   2   The Harvest Report uses the word "crisis" five times, and the word "response" (in the sense of directed reciprocity) eleven times. The Commission's summary uses neither.

   3   The Harvest Report uses the term "violence" nine times with respect to the behavior of the police and the terms "retaliation" nine times, "irrationality" three times, "overreaction" five times, and "breakdown" (of discipline) seven times. None of the above terms appear, with respect to the police, in the Commission's

account, except for the expression "retributive action," once, and the term "overresponse," twice.

4 Conversely, the Commission's summary uses the expressions "cumulation" (of grievances) five times, and "reservoir" (of grievances) also five times. Neither of these terms appears in the Harvest Report.

5 The Commission's summary makes unspecific references to (mounting) "tensions" eighteen times, and two further references to a "disturbed social atmosphere."

The Harvest Report uses the word "tension" four times, three of which are references to relations between specific antagonists.

III The Harvest Report presents the riots as a phase in the increasing politicalization of a social movement. The Commission's summary gives an administrative overview of the riots as external events.

1 The Harvest Report applies technical terms to characterize the riots as collective behavior: "collective rationality," "collective purpose," "coherence," "solidarity," and the like. This terminology does not appear in the Commission's report.

2 Assertions are made in the Harvest Report concerning Negro youths as a rising social force: their weight in numbers, their racial pride, increasing politicalization, blocked political access (lack of representation), and their predominant role in disorders.

Except for the first two points, these features do not appear in the Commission's Report, and even these (numerical preponderance, racial pride) appear as isolated findings.

3 Certain conceptual distinctions of the macrolevel type are introduced and applied in the Harvest Report, but not in the Commission's Report:

a The introduction of a historical–comparative perspective.

b The global characterization of the riots with respect to their degree of political content.

c Contextual characterizations of the riots (e.g.,
"stable" neighborhoods versus those composed of
migrants), introduced as determinants of political
awareness in the ghettos.

d Summary characterizations of city elites' attitudes
with respect to racial issues as liberal, conservative,
and moderate or pluralist.

e The classification of the short-run consequences of
the riots in terms of efforts at change and of racial
polarization.

4 Conversely, the Commission's summary presents the dis-
tribution(s) of the 1967 disorders, with respect to the
following features: location, size of community, timing,
extent of damage, and numbers of people involved. Similarly, the development of violence is sketched in the
following physical terms: timing (times of day, days of the
week), temperatures, numbers of people on the streets,
acceleration to peak, physical forms, and duration of violence. Nothing comparable to those points appears in the
Harvest Report.

5 The Commission's overview includes a section on the
efficacy of selected federal programs (manpower, education, housing, welfare, and community action programs)
in certain cities. (Efficacy is determined in terms of the
proportion of administratively defined eligibles that were
reached.) Nothing comparable appears in the Harvest
Report. The antipoverty program is discussed in general
terms, but only with respect to its potential for the political development of blacks.

6 The Commission's Report discusses the riots and riot
damages in terms of the administrative costs that they
cause, and in terms of the proportion of damaged busi-
nesses that had reopened since. Similarly, it chronicles
the postriot efforts undertaken to prepare municipal
capacities to control further disorders.

The Harvest Report does not contain treatments of
these topics.

This listing of syndromes could readily be extended further. Our point has been to illustrate the nature of the observations on which the general characterizations are built.

PART III: GRADUATE TRAINING IN APPLIED SOCIOLOGY

The Sociology Department of the University of Pittsburgh has established an experimental training program with the help of an NSF grant. A candidate for the M.A. or PH.D. must spend additional time in training toward a special certificate in applied sociology. The hope is that such a certificate would give him additional chances for employment by government agencies, private industry, civic groups, and unions.

The candidate will have to satisfy the requirements for the regular degree. However, within the choices left open by the departmental regulations, the applied program is likely to add specific requirements for full training in research methodology.

The applied program is under the direct supervision of a coordinator who is a junior faculty member. The job of the coordinator is half-time, and he reports to a special executive committee of the department under the chairmanship of a senior member. The assistants in the program and a representative of the students are members of the committee.

The program provides a number of special courses which are required of all students in the program. At the core of these courses is a central seminar in which "a theory of applications" is developed. The seminar is based on a text under this name which has been developed jointly with the ONR project of Columbia University. A first version of this text is about to be published with the expectation that it will be revised and enlarged as Pittsburgh acquires more experience. Part One of this chapter is an example of the kind of "doctrine" that is being developed.

In addition to the expository aspects of this seminar, a number of training devices are being developed. Thus, for instance, each student has to find some organization in Pittsburgh that does social research, and then write a detailed description of one of its specific studies. Each student must also work with one issue of a sociological journal and consider possible applications to which each article in the issue (be it empirical or theoretical) could conceivably be put. The seminar provides experience with respect to applications for research grants. An appropriate "request for proposals" emanating from the government is distributed to the students and each is requested to write out a proposal in all the specified details.

The seminar reviews the literature on the history of applied research, its relation to basic research, and the debates that have surrounded it over the last twenty years. Ethical problems are reviewed with special emphasis on needed research that does not get any financing due to the prevailing power structure. For the students, the writing of such reviews constitutes an exercise in the preparation of reports. In addition, local faculty members (e.g., from the school of business administration), who engage in occasional consultations, are asked to discuss their experiences with the seminar, and these experiences are then jointly analyzed and reviewed.

Other special courses are slowly being developed. Thus, for instance, a term course on research agencies, regarded from the point of view of organizational sociology, is offered periodically, as well as a term course on the applications of social theory. Further courses include a sequence on the history, planning, and utilization of the various Pittsburgh Area Studies, and a course on the utilization of evaluation studies.

The coordinator arranges with faculty members who give substantive courses on, for example, urban sociology or race relations, to devote part of the time to the applied aspect of their field. Students are encouraged to take research courses given in professional schools of social work, public health, or others disciplines. It is hoped that the program, which is now under the Department of Sociology, will become a universitywide arrangement.

A series of lectures is arranged every year in which employers of social scientists tell about their problems and experiences. These lectures are preceded by meetings of the students to get acquainted with the area on which the speaker will talk. In the days after the guest lecture, discussions are held as to what can be learned from this experience.

Each student must take an internship, in most cases during a summer period. All faculty members help the coordinator to provide such opportunities. If the internships are in the Pittsburgh area, the students periodically meet a faculty member to coordinate their practical experience with their systematic education. Students who take their internship outside the city report to the department upon their return.

All students have to file a written final report on their work. A special departmental committee reviews these reports and is gradually developing general guidelines. Many aspects, such as the arrangements and the organizational contact between sponsor and university, are tentative. An effort is made to accumulate knowledge on internship problems, similar to the codified experiences of the British technical colleges on the education of engineers.

Each student is required to become thoroughly acquainted with one specific subject matter from the point of view of social science utilization; for instance, medical sociology, education for underprivileged children, old-age problems, and sociological legislative aspects of unemployment.

The format of the whole program is in a small way similar to the proposal for a graduate school of applied social sciences contained in Chapter XII of the report by the National Academy of Science on the "Behavioral and Social Sciences" (1969).[2] This plan was in turn fashioned after one developed at Columbia for a "Professional School for Training in Social Research" (1950).[3] The latter document was prepared with the help of a Ford Foundation grant in anticipation of what later became the Ford Center for Advanced Study in the Behavioral Sciences (which, however, took quite a different turn).

In this first proposal, special emphasis was placed on the use of case studies: this emphasis is now revived very strongly in the Pittsburgh program. The role of case studies is twofold. Inasmuch as they already exist, they permit a detailed discussion of the whole utilization process in its cognitive as well as in its organizational aspects. But the collection of new case studies is also an important educational device. In addition to brief reviews of ongoing applied research, some students may select a particular situation for thorough study. This can constitute their main work to obtain the certificate and sometimes even a Ph.D. Thus, the collection of case studies that can be used for teaching purposes is steadily increased. The development of this case study program is assigned as a special duty to a senior member of the executive committee.

[2]Now published commercially under this title by Prentice-Hall.
[3]Reprinted in Paul F. Lazarsfeld "Qualitative Analysis," Chapter XVIII. Alin & Bacon, Boston 1972.

Working up cases with the help of students is a difficult task, which undoubtedly has been best developed and described by the Harvard Business School. However, there is a difference between the Harvard and the Pittsburgh case studies. At Harvard they are mainly used for leadership training. Therefore, general managerial problems are described in detail and the students in the program are asked to discuss various solutions to the problem. In Pittsburgh the whole utilization cycle from problem to final action has to be described, analyzed, and discussed. Our idea is not to develop leadership but to train expert sociologists who can understand all phases of applied research and be on an equal plane in their relations with lawyers, consulting engineers, and other professionals likely to be involved in a utilization episode. Of course, the sociologist himself can appear in a variety of roles: as consultant in nonacademic employment, as expert witness, as director of his own or a university-affiliated research bureau, or as an exhorter of the public and its elected representatives in favor of a specific course of action. An applied training program has to prepare its students for all these roles. Some role-playing analogous to the law school moot course might be appropriate, but this has not yet been tried in the Pittsburgh program.

CHAPTER SIX

Four for the Seesaw

Reflections on the Reports of Four Colleagues Concerning Their Experiences as Presidential Commissioners

———————————— RAYMOND W. MACK ————————————

Northwestern University

Four distinguished sociologists have served both their profession and their country by responding to the call for service on Presidential Commissions. These four scholars have now reported to us what they have experienced in their roles as Presidential Commissioners. It is now our turn—and our obligation—to ask ourselves: what have we learned?

One is tempted to catalogue provocative observations, such as Charles Westoff's statement that "Euphemism is the language of public policy." One is further tempted to wander off on his own mission of original research and analysis. I, for example, am fascinated by this question: with an entire Presidential Commission and staff available, what was it about our colleague, Otto Larsen, that made him the most desirable target for a cream pie in the face? One ponders. Having sneaked in those two observations, I shall foreswear this line of inquiry.

Instead, I shall try to organize my observations around three themes.

First, what generalizations can we make as we review the analyses presented to us by Larsen, Ohlin, Short, and Westoff? The range of topics is impressive enough to provide us with a challenge—law enforcement and the administration of justice, population growth and the American future, obscenity and pornography, and the causes and prevention of violence. Since the aim of theory is the explanation of data, and theory works by abstracting and generalizing from observations, we must ask what observations we find across the range of times and topics represented in these reports.

Second, we should address a few nagging questions of the kind that haunt one after he has read these reports of sociologists in action. I have admiration and respect for all four of the authors, but I am anxious about sociologists in general when we are called on as professionals to apply our discipline for the public good.

Third, I shall presume to offer a few prescriptions. Surely one important reason for reviewing the experience of our colleagues is to enable us to ask what we might do better, and how we might go about improving our performance.

First, then, a few generalizations.

GENERALIZATIONS

(1) Each of the four commissioners concludes that the experience was worthwhile, and (2) that such service is an appropriate and worthwhile use of a sociologist's time and skills. These seemingly unimportant generalizations have significance to us as professionals. Given the arid White House soil on which the sociologists' seeds were cast, one might well have expected them to be embittered, and to urge us, their colleagues, not to squander our time and energy in compiling reports that may engender no action beyond an expression of presidential disagreement with the findings. Yet each of the four participant observers is convinced that service by sociologists on Presidential Commissions is good, not only for the Commission, but for the discipline, even though every one of these reports describes the outcome of the Commission's effort in terms of disappointment or failure.

Ohlin stated, "The executive director of the Commission, James Vorenberg, in a recent article in Atlantic magazine, reviewed developments in the five years following the submission of the Commission report. His review expresses considerable disappointment with the excessive law and order preoccupations of policies and funding decisions within LEAA." Short concluded that ". . . we need to be much more skilled, we need much more highly developed data bases, and we need organization and sophistication in matters of government and the law if we are to be effective." Larsen's statement that "The Commission recommends that federal, state, and local legislation prohibiting the sale, exhibition, or distribution of sexual materials to consenting adults should be repealed," was accompanied by nine summary statements in support of this recommendation, six of which drew directly from the empirical studies of the Commission. In reviewing the impact of that data-based recommendation, Larsen concluded, "Therein lies the Commission failure, for the moment at least."

Westoff's experience was that, "The President's response, issued in May 1972, was a disappointment at every level. After some acclaim for the importance of the research for government planning, the President reiterated his personal opposition to abortion and disagreed with the recommendation that contraceptive information and services be made available to minors, on the grounds that this would weaken the family. No attention at all was directed to the basic analysis of the costs and benefits of population growth and the conclusion that population stabilization was desirable."

It is apparent that the findings and recommendations of Presidential Commissions are not respected at the top levels of government; too frequently, the fate of scholars who devote part of their professional lives to such efforts is to see their findings and recommendations ignored or rejected. "The loss, in my judgment, was not the failure to adopt a particular set of recommendations, or even the harsh criticism of the research procedures and findings. It was, rather, the failure of *The Report*, for the time being at least, to penetrate the policy realm with the principle that empirical research is relevant."

Our first generalization, that scholars experienced in the work of Presidential Commissions believe that the effort is worthwhile, may not carry as much weight in the profession as our second generalization, that the reward for such public service may be disappointment and rejection, because our third generalization is that throughout the four reports, we find evidence of great reluctance on the part of sociologists to contribute to the work of Presidential Commissions. Short states that ". . . my first and immediate reaction was to dismiss it as a desperate and futile political gesture. . . . Furthermore, I had only recently resigned from the Graduate Deanship of my university and I was looking forward to the opportunity to complete long delayed research and writing projects." Ohlin reports that "The small number of sociologists was a matter of concern to me and to the executive director as well. The chief obstacle to recruiting knowledgable sociologists as staff members was that recruitment began in October 1965, after the academic year was already underway. Academic and other professional or personal commitments prevented those invited from joining the Washington staff and performing other than consultant roles. We were also unable at that time to find sociologists with training in criminology in other government agencies who could be freed on loan to the Commission for the duration of its work." In assessing Ohlin's statement about the chief obstacle (recruiting in *October*), it is worth noting that Short reports great difficulty in recruiting during *July* and *August*, and Westoff says that he had difficulty in assembling a staff, "a task not made any easier by the fact that *June* is too late in the year to recruit academic people." It may well be that there is really no appropriate season for recruiting people who do not want to be recruited.

There are several obvious hypotheses to account for the difficulty in recruiting sociologists for the work of Presidential Commissions. Such work disrupts whatever plans and schedule a scholar may have. It disrupts not only one's work life, but one's familial and social life. It threatens because it casts the sociologist among strangers in an unfamiliar work environment with ill-defined rules. It offers hard work under severe time pressures, and its rewards are dubious.

But no matter how many such explanations we generate, the fact remains that the legal profession is organized to respond to such challenges and we are not. There is little use in our complaining about the lack of consideration of social science knowledge in legislative, administrative, and judicial decisions if we are not prepared to be on call when our expertise is requested. Listen to Short: "It is important to note the crucial importance of *early* discussions concerning the operation and the focus of the commission. The choice of a director, his choice of personnel and their ready availability, greatly influenced task specification as well as task performance in the division of labor of the Commission." If we believe that our discipline can contribute to public policy, if we care about being heard and about being effective, the most poignant passage in all these pages is from Short: "A few contacts with social scientists had been made before I began working with the Commission, but our colleagues were difficult to recruit and slow to come aboard; most had other commitments which interfered with full-time Commission service, few could spend much time in the Commission offices. The lawyers, however, were there."

Other generalizations can, of course, be abstracted from these four rich sets of data, but it seems that these three are the ones most crucial for us to assess as members of a professional association: (1) service on a Presidential Commission is deemed worthwhile for the discipline and for society by those who have experienced it; (2) the probability is high of a disappointing response or no response from the White House to social science findings and recommendations; and (3) if we believe the first generalization, we must ask why we are such reluctant handmaidens to public policy-makers, and ask how we can deliver a more effective response to calls for social science contributions to governance.

Let me turn now to two questions that these four reports raise.

QUESTIONS

(1) Why are we not as well organized as the legal profession to respond to requests for public service?

A national legal firm such as Sidley and Austin will have the firm's work reassigned and some of its best young people in an office in Washington within days of a request from the White House. Should not a national university such as Stanford be equally well prepared and equipped to meet such a challenge?

In contrasting lawyers with social scientists on the National Commission on the Causes and Prevention of Violence, Short says

They were accustomed to the pressure-cooker atmosphere of crash preparations, and they were more familiar with government operations, and with Washington bureaucracies. They were, further, accustomed to the quick gathering and assimilation of concrete facts and their use in advocacy, in contrast to the more deliberative style of research and preference for abstract theoretical formulations of academics. The lawyer's approach to problems was generally preferred by the commissioners who felt compelled to marshal facts quickly, in order to reach conclusions and make recommendations—at least plausible, if not entirely acceptable conclusions and recommendations—to the President and to the public. It was they, after all, far more than the staff, who were 'on the line' with respect to reputation and constituencies represented.

I include this quote to emphasize the fact that we as a profession are on the line. If it is clear that sociologists respect the dedication and delivery of scholars such as Larsen, Ohlin, Short, and Westoff, other sociologists will make the sacrifices necessary to serve the discipline in the public interest.

(2) Why are we not better prepared to answer pressing questions of great concern about our own data base—our own society?

Sociologists do have a point of view, a frame of reference, a way of looking at social life. We should be useful for both of the standard assignments given to Presidential Commissions: fact-finding and explanation, or analysis. But when we are asked for generalizations about behavior as central to the interests of our discipline as crime, violence, or population growth, our initial response is to retreat from the hazards of theoretical generalization and to seek security in the field, designing research and gathering data. We sound like the last paragraph of a standard journal article: "Further research is needed."

Articles in the American Journal of Sociology, Social Forces, the American Political Science Review, the Behavioral Scientist, the American Sociological Review, and the like often end with several paragraphs detailing the inadequacies of the author's research design and execution and denying any intention on his part to generalize about the findings, that is, to theorize. Perhaps we could inaugurate a FRIN-convention. Were editors to agree to print, in block caps, at the end of each article where the author deemed it appropriate, the letters, F.R.I.N., we would all understand that further research is needed. The deletion of the several paragraphs per article devoted to a discussion of this fact might allow room for another article per issue. Better yet, editors might demand that each author have a try at a careful, imaginative interpretation of the likely meanings of his data.

I am, of course, not speaking against empiricism, but I am worrying about our theory-shyness. We are probably better at theorizing than we give ourselves credit for. Professor Ohlin says:

> Social science concepts, theories, and general perspectives were probably of greater utility to the staff and the Commission in forming the final recommendations than the inputs from new knowledge development efforts funded by the Commission as research projects. Advice from the technical advisory panel and other consultants, together with staff surveys of the literature, constituted the primary resource for staff in assessing the state of knowledge in the field. Theories that seemed to be supported by this current knowledge were then relied upon to suggest action implications. Thus, consultant papers, fact-finding by staff, and the results of research projects served primarily to provide supportive data and persuasive arguments for recommendations and general strategies for crime control and prevention, which had already been tentatively formulated by drawing on expert social science and professional opinion. Existing social science theories and data were drawn upon to formulate broad general strategies in the prevention and control of crime. The staff then developed more detailed recommendations which would serve to implement these strategies through new public policies, allocation of public resources, and proposals for change in the specific operation and organization of criminal justice agencies.
>
> In other words, the greatest strength of the social science contribution lay in providing sensitizing concepts and theories which oriented the search for solutions of the crime problem along certain paths.

The reason I did not include this question under my generalizations is simple: most of the evidence from these reports indicates that under the pressure of a direct question about human social behavior, we are more often ready to initiate a research project than to answer the question. As Larsen says:

> . . . the state of the social sciences as perceived at that time equipped us to do what was essentially abstracted empirical research, but did not equip us to shape the research around policy alternatives. Policy was something you took up after you had done the research.
>
> Here is where I now see that we missed a rare opportunity to link social research to social policy in an effective manner. We failed because we did not turn our tools first to an empirical analysis of policy options so that the remainder of the research on effects, etc., would

illuminate the costs and consequences of realistic alternative courses of action. In short, we did not have a policy-research theory to guide our strategy.

Both of these questions deserve thoughtful attention from all of us: (1) Why are we not ready as a profession to respond positively to requests for public service?; and (2) Why are we not ready, as social scientists, to answer with confidence pressing questions about the social order?

Let me turn, in conclusion, to a few prescriptions.

PRESCRIPTIONS

(1) We should encourage and promote the use of younger social scientists on Presidential Commissions.

There is an establishment. We hope that it is an establishment of demonstrated competence. The best known sociologists should be those who have published frequently and whose work has been of the solid quality that enables others to build on it. And these sociologists are in a position to know who are the most promising and competent young scholars they have seen, taught, and worked with during the preceding five years. These young sociologists, recently out of graduate school, have three invaluable attributes that distinguish them from the more established sociologists most likely to be sought for Commission work: (1) they are less entangled in dissertation advising, university administration, and national committee work—in other words, they are more readily available; (2) they are more up-to-date (whether or not their establishment sponsors would like to admit it) on recent research methods, recent research findings, and new theoretical ideas (we all know that one is never again as well read as on the day when he writes his qualifying examinations); and (3) younger scholars have more to gain in developing their own careers from participating in such a national arena as is offered by the Presidential Commission. For the beginning social scientist, service on a Presidential Commission may be seen not as a burden but as an opportunity—for access to data, for significant publication, and for professional visibility.

(2) Short calls our attention to a serious shortcoming we suffer in our relations with the wider society, briefly: "We continue to write primarily for each other and for our students."

Scholars are averse to discussing public relations. Nonetheless, we should recognize that a major difficulty we face in seeking support for our work stems from the poor public relations that social science has with two publics: government officials and the voting citizenry. No small part of this problem derives from labels; our poor public relations flow, in part, from the semantics of scholarship. If, indeed, we know what we are doing while the legislators and the general citizenry do not, it might be wise for us to tell them about it in their vocabulary instead of insisting that it is their obligation to learn ours. Were it my responsibility to defend before a Congressional committee the budget of the Committee on Research Training in the Behavioral Sciences, my first wish would be that we could change its name to the Committee for a Better Understanding of Poverty, Racism, and Urbanization. Although this may offend some of our colleagues, will it offend them as much as not having any financial support for their work?

Our cause is ill served by our insistence on the distinction between basic, or pure (good), research as opposed to applied, or noncumulative (second-rate), research. This distinction is senseless in the behavioral sciences, but attempts to convince my colleagues of this may not be a worthwhile expenditure of time. I am even more dubious that it is worthwhile to try to explain to the taxpayers who support us why we think the distinction is so important. Since I do not know of any research methodologies that are applied as opposed to other methods that are pure, nor of any applied theories readily distinguishable from basic theories, it would seem constructive for us to think lovingly of the purity of our research and speak immodestly of its potential applicability.

(2) I offer my final prescription in an attempt to ease the discomfort of those who worry about the difference between basic and applied research, and because I believe that it promises to minimize the theoretical waste that indeed can accompany social-problem-oriented fact-gathering. Each Presidential Commission report should be followed by a volume on continuities in social research. Both those sociologists who participated in the Commission and others who did not should be asked what the findings imply for our understanding of the human group. We owe that to ourselves. The Merton and Kitt work,[1] capitalizing on the data base pro-

---

[1]Robert K. Merton and Alice S. Kitt, "Contributions to the Theory of Reference Group Behavior," in *Continuities in Social Research: Studies in the Scope and Method of "The American Soldier,"* edited by Robert K. Merton and Paul F. Lazarsfeld. (Glencoe, Ill.: The Free Press, 1950).

vided by *The American Soldier*, is exemplary of what I mean by this prescription. The Executive Office of the American Sociological Association, through our Publications Committee and our Council, should organize and implement the commissioning of such analytic volumes. In this way, we may not only serve our society through social science, but also improve the quality of our social science for society.

CHAPTER SEVEN

Social Knowledge and Public Policy

Sociological Perspectives on Four Presidential Commissions

————— ROBERT K. MERTON —————

Columbia University

HISTORICAL PRELIMINARIES

Commissions—in the broad sense of a collegial body of persons charged by an authority with designated activity and purpose—have long been an element in governance. Perhaps the most famous and the most effective commissions have been the Royal Commissions of Inquiry in Britain, which came into their own in the nineteenth century as "favored instruments leading to major advances in social legislation, such as the Factory

The writing of this chapter was supported in part by NSF grant SSH71-01834 A01 from the RANN (Research Applied to National Needs) Program of NSF to the Center for Advanced Study in the Behavioral Sciences and in part by NSF grant GS 33359X2 to the Program in the Sociology of Science, Columbia University. Helpful criticism was given me by Robert Dahl, Cynthia Epstein and fellow Fellows at the Center: Graham Allison, Robert Darnton, Irving Janis, Martin Krieger, James March, Arnold Thackray, and Edward Tufte.

Acts."[1] And perhaps the most generous and surely the most notable tribute to the character and accomplishments of the royal commissions is
found in these familiar words:

> The social statistics of Germany and the rest of Continental
> Western Europe are, by comparison with those of England, wretchedly
> compiled. But they raise the veil just enough to let us catch a glimpse
> of the Medusa head behind it. We should be appalled at the state of
> things at home, if, as in England, our governments and parliaments
> appointed periodically commissions of inquiry into economic condi-
> tions; if these commissions were armed with the same plenary powers
> to get at the truth; if it was possible to find for this purpose men as
> competent, as free from partisanship and respect of persons as are the
> English factory-inspectors, her medical reporters on public health, her
> commissioners of inquiry into the exploitation of women and children,
> into housing and food.[2]

This unstinted praise of the composite integrity, truth-telling, and
capability for social investigation of commissions of inquiry appears in
Karl Marx's *Capital*—in the celebrated preface to the first German edition. Evidently, the founder of modern Communism, the prime contribu-
tor to an early sociology of knowledge, and the pitiless critic of bourgeois
society thought it possible for men "to get at the truth" about social and
economic conditions obtaining in that society and to record part of that
truth in the form of "social statistics." As Marx explains, the truth was
being searched out by royal commissions and others at work in the service
of that dispossessing instrument of the ruling class, the bourgeois English
State.

Not, of course, that Marx ascribed the integrity of these critical investigators to lofty motives. What is more interesting and more nearly in
accord with his general doctrine is that he saw this institutionalized pattern of truth-telling as itself socially induced. It is identified as an expression of class interest in a particular historical context. The American Civil

---

[1]Charles J. Hanser. *Guide to Decision: The Royal Commission* (Totowa, N.J.: The Bed-
minster Press, 1965); see also Harvey C. Mansfield. "Commissions, Government." *International Encyclopedia of the Social Sciences* (New York: Macmillan Co. and The Free Press,
1968), Vol. III, pp. 13–18.

[2]Karl Marx. *Capital* (Moscow: Foreign Languages Publishing House, 1959), Vol. I,
p. 9.

War had "sounded the tocsin for the European working class," just as the American War of Independence had done for the European middle class.

> In England the progress of social disintegration is palpable. . . . A-
> part from higher motives, therefore, their own most important interests
> dictate to the classes that are for the nonce the ruling ones, the removal
> of all legally removable hindrances to the free development of the
> working-class.[3]

In short extension and paraphrase, Marx is, in effect, advancing the interesting idea that under certain conditions, self-interest, collective and individual, can make for truth-seeking and truth-telling just as, under other conditions, it can and notoriously does make for deliberate lying as well as unwitting deception, both of self and of others.

Commissions of inquiry have not been confined to England. From the beginning, Presidents of the United States have also had their commissions. Washington began with a commission to look into the Whiskey Rebellion: ever since, Presidents or Congress have instituted one or another kind of commission, at first sporadically and then, in this century, at a greatly quickened pace.[4]

Mansfield has instructively proposed three conjoint criteria for sorting out types of commissions. First, in terms of duration, ranging from "bodies convened *ad hoc* to deal with a specific situation" to those permanently established. Second, in terms of their varying overt purposes, among them arbitration, regulation, operation of public enterprise, advice-giving, investigation of a major historical event (e.g., assassination of

---

[3]Ibid. p. 9.

[4]No exhaustive counts exist, but it is said that Hoover appointed about 60 commissions and advisory boards during the first year-and-a-half of his presidency; Franklin Roosevelt, more than a hundred in his first two terms; Truman, a mere twenty or so during nearly eight years in office with Eisenhower proceeding at a Truman-like rate during his first term. As we might suppose, the commissions were of varying scope, duration, intensity and consequence but little is known about them through systematic investigation. The estimates of numbers are assembled by Alan L. Dean, "*Ad hoc* Commissions for Policy Formulation?" in Thomas E. Cronin and Sanford D. Greenberg, *The Presidential Advisory System* (New York: Harper & Row, 1969), pp. 101–116. However, the estimates evidently include a good many advisory bodies other than Presidential Commissions, strictly so-called. Popper has compiled a list of these in recent administrations: 11 for Truman, 4 for Eisenhower, 4 for Kennedy, 20 for Johnson, and 5 during Nixon's first two years in office. Frank Popper, *The President's Commissions* (New York: Twentieth Century Fund, 1970, Appendix 1).

a president), and of most immediate interest to us, commissions charged with the study, planning, and recommendation of public policy. Third, commissions can be considered in terms of their "latent functions, notably, bargaining [among disparate interests], public education, delay, patronage, appeasement, frustration of opposition to current policy, and rubber-stamping."[5] From the standpoint of structure, as Mansfield also notes, the commission form is admirably suited to serving a representational function, by providing for voice in its deliberations to a diversity of distinct and often opposed interests. The extent to which commissions have actually been made up of members strongly opposed in interests and values is quite another, politically significant matter.

This chapter deals with a quartet of American Presidential Commissions, appointed for a limited time within the last years for the announced purpose of formulating plans and recommendations for public policy bearing on four distinct sets of socially defined problems in American society. Beyond their announced purpose, as we will see, these *ad hoc* commissions had a variety of latent functions and dysfunctions for diverse social formations. To meet its charge, each of the commissions arranged for research projects and programs, consisting principally of social research of one description or another.

This practice of social investigation is in direct continuity with what had become a tradition for the British Royal Commissions. These regularly provided for inquiry that would "make for a definitive determination of controversial facts and [so it was said] for a trustworthy judgment on a complex public problem."[6] In turn, the Royal Commissions had an emerging tradition of empirical social investigation to draw upon. As Stephen Cole has shown, the statistical and social science associations in Britain that had come into being before the middle of the nineteenth century were largely activated by concern with social reform. With increasing regularity, they fostered or actually mounted empirical investigations of crime, poverty, prison life, factory conditions, and kindred problems. Even before applied social research became more fully institutionalized in the form of providing for a trained full-time paid staff, such research

---

[5]Mansfield, op. cit., pp. 13–14; see also Daniel Bell. "Government by Commission," *The Public Interest* No. 3 (Spring 1966), pp 3–9.

[6]Hanser, op. cit., 220. It should be emphasized that Royal Commissions and Presidential Commissions have only a cousinly resemblance, structural and functional. For contrasts as well as similarities between them, see Popper, op. cit., pp. 50–54.

was being carried forward by a variety of (sometimes voluntary and often self-taught) investigators: actuaries, army officers, businessmen, civil servants, clergy, physicians, and, tellingly enough, early in the period, only a sprinkling of professors. Cole goes on to observe that the great bulk of these *de facto* social researchers were in professions that provided them with access to statistics institutionally generated by hospitals, philanthropic organizations, the courts, prisons, and various other agencies of government.[7]

Marx was thus merely being observant when he praised the social statistics and other social data being compiled before his eyes in England. It was these data that would enable him and others to reconstruct crucial aspects of the English social reality, to get "upon the right track for the discovery of the natural laws of its movement." It was for reasons such as this, writes Marx, that "I have given so large a space in this volume to the history, the details, and the results of English factory legislation."[8] And an abundant space it is. No one has yet inventoried the whole of the official reports by commissions of inquiry, factory inspectors, public health inspectors, and the other Blue books, which Marx drew upon in the *Capital.* But his careful citation practices, more meticulous than those adopted by most of us pedantically inclined academicians, afford a clue to the scale on which he made use of the researches stemming from these sources. A small sampling of his liberal citations is enough to serve us here.

The 60,000-word monograph entitled "Machinery and Modern Industry," which constitutes the celebrated Chapter XV of the first volume

[7]Stephen Cole. "Continuity and Institutionalization in Science: A Case Study of a Failure," in Anthony Oberschall, ed. *The Establishment of Empirical Sociology: Studies in Continuity, Discontinuity, and Institutionalization* (New York: Harper & Row, 1972), pp 73–129; see also the paper by David Elesh, pp. 31–72 in the same volume, "The Manchester Statistical Society: A Case Study of Discontinuity in the History of Empirical Social Research." As Paul F. Lazarsfeld reports in his Foreword to that volume, these and other historical and sociological studies of the early period of empirical social research derived from a graduate seminar at Columbia which he and I gave jointly in the 1960s. But what Lazarsfeld characteristically does not go on to report, his conviction about the potential significance of this subject ran deeper than mine. It was he, rather than I, who instituted a series of investigation of one or another aspect of the subject by Oberschall, Bernard-Pierre Lécuyer, Terry Clark, Suzanne Shad, and others. For two other instructive inquiries, see Nathan Glazer. "The Rise of Social Research in Europe," in Daniel Lerner, ed. *The Human Meaning of the Social Sciences* (New York: Meridian, 1959); and Philip Abrams. *The Origins of British Sociology, 1834–1914* (Chicago: University of Chicago Press, 1968).

[8]*Capital*, pp. 9–10.

of *Capital*, contains some 240 footnotes. About a sixth of these are given over to developing points in the text or to demolishing *Bêtes noires* (such as Malthus and Ure); the remaining 200 or so are used to indicate the sources of the evidence and ideas that he introduces in the text.[9] The arithmetic of these citations summarizes the copious extent to which Marx drew upon the investigations recorded in those reports of parliamentary commissions and other official bodies, known from their dark blue paper covers simply as the Blue books.

Of the approximately 200 citations of all sources, including ancient, medieval, and modern writings, 138 (or more than two-thirds) were to Blue books of one sort of another: 70 referred to Reports of Inspectors of Factories; 45 to Reports of Royal Commissions; 11 to Reports on Public Health; 9 to the Census (primarily of 1861); and 3 to other Blue books (such as the Statistical Abstract of the United Kingdom).[10]

[9]His collaborator and editor was altogether aware of the diverse functions served by Marx's use of quotations and citations, principally in footnotes. In his Preface to the English edition of *Capital*, Engels itemizes these functions, hinting at Marx's interest in what was to become the sociology of knowledge and at his deep commitment to the rights of private intellectual property. Following the style of Marx's own practice, one should fully quote Engels's observations to this effect: "A word respecting the author's [this being, of course, Marx's] method of quoting may not be out of place. In the majority of cases, the quotations serve, in the usual way, as documentary evidence in support of assertions made in the text. But in many instances, passages from economic writers are quoted [n.b.] in order to indicate when, where, and by whom a certain proposition was for the first time clearly enunciated. This is done in cases where the proposition quoted is of importance as being a more or less adequate expression of the conditions of social production and exchange prevalent at the time, and quite irrespective of Marx's recognition, or otherwise, of its general validity. These quotations, therefore, supplement the text by a running commentary taken from the history of the science." *Capital, op. cit.*, 5. Marx's practice generalized would greatly extend the current use of citation analysis for tracing genealogies of ideas.

[10]England, taken by Marx as "the classic ground" of "the capitalist mode of production" and therefore "used as the chief illustration in the development of my theoretical ideas," provided other sources of data about its social reality that could be utilized both by critics and defenders of that society. On a half-dozen occasions in the same Chapter XV, Marx drew upon papers and publications by the emerging societies for the advancement of social science. He notes in a "Report of the Social Science Congress, at Edinburgh," October 1863, that "In England women are still occasionally used instead of horses for hauling canal boats." (*Capital*, p. 394). Similarly, he refers the reader to "the speech of N. W. Senior at the seventh annual congress of The National Association for the Promotion of Social Science," 1863, which deals with "the very advantageous results of combining gymnastics-. . . with compulsory education for factory children and pauper scholars." Marx thus provides eloquent testimony to the ways in which authentic social reportage and social science can provide subversive evidence about the social reality, a secular version of the doctrine that the truth shall help to make you free.

Never before, surely, and probably never since, have the reports of governmental commissions been put to more consequential use.

These few scattered observations on commissions of inquiry in an earlier time and another place are perhaps enough to provide perspective and distance as we examine the use of research by commissions in our own time and place. The observations remind us of the following:

1 Governmental commissions of inquiry are themselves an historically evolving social form for discovering or systematically describing selected aspects of a social reality.

2 Commissions are both producers and consumers of social research.

3 The institutionalization of procedures for undertaking research on behalf of commissions engaged in recommending public policy began some time ago and is presumably still in process.

4 The use of that research need not be confined to its utilization by the commissions inaugurating it.

5 As the historic case of Marx emphatically proclaims, the results of authentic social inquiry can be utilized by people sharply differing in political commitments from those of the commissioners or the investigators.

FOUR PRESIDENTIAL COMMISSIONS OF INQUIRY

As a sociological understanding of social institutions and collective behavior would lead us to expect, national commissions of inquiry are created by the President or the Congress or both in response to their reading of the social and political temper of the times, current and prospective. Commissions are usually established in Times of Trouble. (That is, one supposes, why there have been so many of them.) The public troubles are sometimes acute, sometimes chronic, and the one kind is frequently superimposed upon the other.

Acute troubles often lead to the formation of commissions to investigate the unique event (as in the case of the Warren Commission). Occasionally, specific events trigger the appointment of a commission to inquire into the enduring problem dramatized by the particular event, as with the National Commission on Violence, instituted in the grim hours after the assassination of Robert Kennedy. When commissions are created to formulate new policies on chronic problems even though there has been no sudden, visible change in actual circumstances, this presumably represents a threshold phenomenon of accumulated troubles (as, for example, with the belated public and institutionalized response to the deterioration of our human and natural environments). Finally, it seems to have been a combination of chronic and acute troubles that led to a commission to examine the socially defined problems of obscenity and pornography, when that age-old continuity of interest in matters judged unchaste was coupled with a conspicuous growth in scale. In all cases, it appears, national commissions are in origin and outcome deeply affected by both actual and perceived climates of public opinion and action.

Whatever their historical origins and their manifest and latent functions, commissions of inquiry are—commissions of inquiry. That is, they are publicly committed to make a search or investigation directed toward uncovering germane information and knowledge; they are, in short, institutionally committed to research. The research may turn out to be sound or specious, wide-ranging or parochial, deeply significant or inconsequential, inspired or pedestrian. But the public commitment being what it is, research there must be. Yet, surprisingly little seems to be systematically known about the ways in which research programs and projects are brought into being by these policy-formulating commissions, how the research is conducted, and most of all, how the results of research relate to the formulation of proposed policy.

It is therefore a rare opportunity to have circumstantial accounts about these matters prepared by sociologists who have played a major role as members of recent Presidential Commissions: Otto Larsen; Lloyd Ohlin; James Short; and Charles Westoff.

Their accounts, written from the perspective of participant-observers, exhibit an interesting symmetry, with a methodological aesthetic all their own. In their role as *participants,* the authors deal principally with sociology *in* the Commissions (i.e., with the use, nonuse, misuse, or pointed absence of sociological knowledge). In their role as *observers,* they deal principally with the sociology *of* the Commissions (i.e., with their origins, structure, dynamics, evolution, and aftermath). That division of the subject provides a ready format for my own observations on what has been reported to us.

THE SOCIOLOGY OF COMMISSIONS

It appears throughout that the variety of social processes, structures, and functions observed in the behavior of the commissions can be related to the variegated problematics of the sociological discipline itself.

Plainly, the commissions exhibit the operation of power structures in the production, use, abuse and nonuse of sociological knowledge. Composed of representatives of various (not, of course, all) constituencies, each commission was bound to experience some degree of internal conflict. From the standpoint of structural analysis, this observed pattern of conflicting perspectives among the commissioners is no mere happenstance. For in a society structurally differentiated as ours is, conflict *must* result from the groundplan of a commission that authentically represents people located in diverse strata and sectors of the social structure, with their distinctive and often incompatible interests and values.

To the extent that the membership of a commission represents the spectrum of major interest groups, this would seem to guarantee a structurally induced strain toward initial conflict and subsequent compromise or continuing stasis. Apparently, it is with commissions as it is with food: the effort to cater to all tastes makes for blandness. Yet, on more than one occasion, through a sociologically interesting process of trade-offs, the commissions came out with strong collective recommendations which individual commissioners were surprised to find themselves endorsing. Some of the recommendations of the Commission on Pornography, for example, were in this special sense spicy rather than bland.

In part, this results from small group processes in continuing or intermittent operation. Processes of polarization, conflict, and mutual accommodation were at work under varying, sometimes ill-understood conditions. But the principal group-induced pressures were generally for compromise. As one observer summed this up, there is apparently nothing like an implacable deadline, as distinct from an ideology, to move a *task-oriented group* toward consensus. In seeming paradox, the commission format providing for minority reports may make for wider consensus than would otherwise obtain. Knowing that the minority can openly dissent, the visible majority may be more agreeable to modifying their position to avoid a scatter of contested recommendations. In turn, the minority report as an avenue of public expression becomes a structural device for avoiding the stasis condition of a hung jury.

Another aspect of the behavior of commissions can be identified from the perspective of a structural sociology focused on organizational constraints and processes of differentiation in groups. One constraint derives from what some of us take to be important variables in group structure and individual membership in groups. These variables can be described as the *expected* (not only the actual) *duration* of a group or organization and the expected duration of the occupancy of a status within a group or organization. Groups differ significantly in this aspect; many have an expectation of indefinitely continuing duration; some have an assigned life span. Memberships in groups differ in the same way: some, as in the case of tenure positions, carry the expectation of indefinitely continued duration; others, as in the case of statutory limits on the holding of office, have a known pending termination. Such socially shared expectations of duration greatly affect the orientations and behavior of members of the group, the workings of authority and power within it, and not least, the social environment in which the group finds its place.[11]

Consequences of the two types of expected duration are repeatedly implied and sometimes expressed in the description of the commissions' behavior. Thus, Lloyd Ohlin notes of the Commission on Law Enforcement and Administration of Justice that "The Chairman, executive Director . . . and many staff members were acutely conscious of the fact that a Presidential Commission has no enduring life and must rely on other established institutions and agencies to implement the results of its work." This sense of the short, more-or-less unhappy life of the Crime Commission, this sense of its expected brief duration, led to a strategy of attempting to involve states and localities in a continuing program. In another connection, Otto Larsen reports that "confidentiality began to disappear completely toward the end of the [Pornography] Commission's life as drafts of reports were circulated," a result that might follow as much from the stage of the work as from the short, remaining duration of the Commission. James Short refers to the substantial effects on the Commission on Violence of Lyndon Johnson's lame-duck incumbency, requiring the research to be carried out and a progress report to be sub-

[11]I have long argued that this is so. See R. K. Merton. (*Social Theory and Social Structure* (New York: The Free Press, 1968, enlarged edition). pp. 365–66; and three of us found it to be so in a study of "planned communities" conducted some time ago: R. K. Merton, P. S. West and M. Jahoda. *Patterns of Social Life: Explorations in the Sociology of Housing* (Columbia University Bureau of Applied Social Research, 1948, mimeo.).

mitted before a new President was inaugurated. The lame-duck pattern is the classical archetype in which the known duration of occupancy of a status operates to affect policy-formation and to make for the decreasingly effective exercise of authority.

Still, if it produces a body of research, the socially consequential life of a commission can extend well beyond its existence as a formally convened body. Long after it has been discharged with presidential (or parliamentary) thanks, the inquiries mounted by the commission can remain consequential, as we noted in the case of the Blue books which the British Museum made available to Marx, and as we can note now, for example, in the case of the Crime Surveys made available by the Crime Commission.

Another important constraint upon the utilization of social research by the commissions was the discordant pacing of empirical social inquiry and of decision-making. The participant-observers uniformly note that the comparatively slow pace of much social research was out of phase with the urgent timetable by which national commissions work. In this regard, nothing much seems to have happened since at least the 1940s (and, one suspects, long before) when a study of policy-oriented research reported that "the tempo of policy decisions and action is often more rapid than the tempo of applied [social] research."[12]

This temporal disjuncture between research and policy-formation sets severe limits upon the possibility that the commissions could draw upon social research for many pertinent problems emerging in their deliberations. All this raises several questions about current practices involving the relations of commissions to research programs. As we have seen, *ad hoc* commissions of inquiry are usually appointed in Times of Trouble. They are to seek out the sources of one or another of the currently defined troubles and to tell us what to do about them. For both manifest and latent political functions, commissions tend to be instituted in politically expedient or politically inevitable times. This should lead us to ask whether those are the best times for investigating (not necessarily recom-

---

[12]R. K. Merton. "The Role of Applied Social Science in the Formation of Policy," *Philosophy of Science* 16 (July 1949), pp. 161–81, reprinted as Chapter 4 in Merton, *The Sociology of Science* (Chicago: University of Chicago Press, 1973), the quotation on p. 88. Since the organizers of this symposium have asked me to draw upon my longstanding (and, I like to think, evolving) perspectives on the connections of social knowledge to the formation of policy, I shall continue to refer to my writings throughout this paper.

mending modes of coping with) the problems in and of our society. It may be, as Edward Tufte has suggested, that the most effective political strategy is to exploit short-run pressures for long-run improvement; the so-called crisis may provide the only chance that will present itself. But although a crisis mentality about a chronic problem provides a politically feasible basis for establishing a Presidential Commission, the same sense of urgency works against doing the careful and considerable research needed then and there. As we learn from the testimony of participant-observers of the research brought into being by an urgent commission, much of it must be piecemeal or otherwise limited by the exigencies of the public business to be transacted.[13]

Since considerations of political expediency—implying political feasibility—are bound to affect the timing of governmentally established commissions, there is reason to argue for the more frequent creation of national commissions by other institutions and associations in the society. Foundations do occasionally provide for such commissions and for programs of research, extending over a period of years, oriented to their requirements. Beyond that, there would seem to be a place for learned societies and professional associations in the social sciences to develop proto-commissions of their own, which would define public issues from their theoretical stance and provide for associated programs of ongoing research oriented to those issues.

I take up only one more item in this incomplete inventory of observations on the sociology *of* commissions which also links up with the role of sociology *in* commissions. Problems in both the microsociology and the macrosociology of scientific knowledge are implicated in the work of commissions.

The participant-observer accounts are rich in detail about the divergence of moral and intellectual perspectives of commissioners and staff drawn from different sectors of the society. Consider only the most conspicuous case: the interaction of the lawyers and the social scientists in trying to shape a knowledge-related set of recommendations.

As has always been the case since it became our capital, Washington is densely populated by lawyers. Presidential Commissions are generally even more so. The Commission on Population is a rare exception. Of its

[13]James March has suggested that research does not always lag behind the knowledge and information requirements for formulating public policy. Research on the genetic effects of radiation, for example, apparently outruns the pace of policy-formation which takes that research into account.

twenty-four members, only a handful were lawyers, and these gained entry chiefly as members of Congress. The other three Commissions more nearly reverted to type. Although the Commission on Pornography also had an unusual number of sociologists—Otto Larsen, Joseph Klapper, Marvin Wolfgang—a third of the eighteen Commissioners had law degrees. Fifteen of the nineteen members of the Crime Commission were lawyers, as were fifteen of twenty-five of the Task Force Directors of the Commission on Violence.

The preponderance of lawyers should come as no surprise: Max Weber had long since remarked on the special availability of lawyers for every arm and function of government. Nor is this merely a result of their lawyerly skills. It also has to do with the structure of their occupation. Far more than, say, physicians or even academics, lawyers can readily detach themselves from their ordinary jobs to take on extraordinary assignments for longer or shorter periods. This eventuates in a tradition of public service within the guild of lawyers that becomes self-perpetuating, in no little part because it is at times greatly rewarded. Lawyers also experience something of role-congruence between the requirements of their occupational roles and the demands of such *ad hoc* units as national commissions.

However, it is not the contrast in detachability of lawyers and academic social scientists, but the differences between them in styles of work, intellectual perspectives, and, specifically, conceptions of evidence that must be noted here. The modes and loci of diverse and sometimes rival professional expertise are themes running throughout the reported behavior of staffs and commissioners. These are perhaps best crystallized in the preference of lawyers for use of sworn eye-witness depositions, and the contrasting preference of sociologists for interviews, social surveys, and other quantitative evidence. These preferences are sustained by a considerable professional apparatus and a not inconsiderable academic apparatus by which the evidence is evaluated. The reward system of science and learning, centered in peer review, reinforces the differential attachment to types of evidence.

An applied sociology of knowledge must take note of such structurally patterned differences in conceptions of what constitutes adequate evidence. It would be of no little interest to mount a research program that systematically compares the scope, relevance, validity, and utility of data which, collected in diverse ways, bear upon the same public issues considered by public commissions and other groups. A next step into the sociology of knowledge would require us to compare the evaluation of these methods by experts drawn from disciplines that have institutionalized distinct methods of gathering and distinct criteria for assessing evidence on the subject.

At any rate, we can earmark the micro- and macrosociology of knowledge as another basic context for that investigation of the behavior and consequences of commissions which constitute the sociology *of* commissions.

SOCIOLOGY IN THE COMMISSIONS

Sociology *in* the Commissions—that is, the actual role of sociological knowledge in the work and the conclusions of the Commissions—provides its own microcosm of the discipline at large.

To the extent that the commissions drew upon sociological knowledge at all, that knowledge was evidently diverse in both general perspective and specific findings. None of the commissions, or their research staffs, confined itself to a single comprehensive and tight-knit paradigm that defined the range of problems and subjects to be investigated in detail and determined how they were to be investigated. Instead, the Commissions, or at least their staffs, were tacitly committed to a pluralistic theoretical orientation. In some degree, this pluralism was probably built into the structure of the Commissions through the appointment of members representing different constituencies with differing cognitive as well as value perspectives. But, in any case, it is apparent that the sociological research for the Commissions did not uniformly or primarily derive from a single theoretical orientation—not functional analysis, symbolic interactionism, or social ecology; not structural analysis, exchange theory, or social dramaturgy. Indeed, not even Marxism.

This kind of theoretical pluralism only reproduces in microcosm the actual and the cognitively appropriate state of the field of sociology itself —and of the behavioral sciences generally. Even to signal the grounds for this statement of preference for a pluralistic rather than monistic structure of sociological knowledge would require us to move far beyond our immediate subject.[14] But it can be argued that differing theoretical orien-

[14]For a statement of these grounds, see R. K. Merton. "Structural Analysis in Sociology," in Peter M. Blau, ed. *Approaches to the Study of Social Structure* (New York: The Free Press, 1975).

tations are useful for an understanding of differing kinds and aspects of sociological and social problems. Whatever the claim to the contrary by advocates of this or that theoretical stance, actual inquiry (and conspicuously so for inquiry aimed at dealing with concrete social problems) requires the use of complementary paradigms and conceptions.

I am aware that, in some quarters, "eclecticism" is an abusive epithet used to designate a shabby, incoherent collection of *ad hoc* interpretations of aspects of reality. The modifier, "mere," is unthinkingly introduced with such frequency that expression becomes telescoped into the composite—"mereclecticism." Yet, the controlled and systematic use of complementary ideas drawn from differing orientations in the form of what can be called "disciplined eclecticism" characterizes much of social science today.[15]

Just as the aggregate of sociologists doing the research for the Commissions adopted a plurality of theoretical orientations, so they also adopted a plurality of methods of inquiry. I shall not dwell here upon the circumstance that different sorts of questions, derived from theoretical constructions or stimulated by empirical observations, call for different sorts of data acquired through diverse methods. It is perhaps enough to note that the plurality of methods employed by the commissions' research staffs for the collection of data and for their ordering and interpretation also provides a replica of what is the collective practice in sociology at large.

The research program of the Commissions provides a miniaturized replica of our discipline in still another aspect: the basic presuppositions involved in the imagery of the sociological knowledge thought necessary for formulating grounded recommendations for action. So far as one can tell, that imagery of the ambiguous relations between knowledge and the formulation of policy entertained by the researchers was not dominated by any of the various, at times simple-minded, positivisms: neither the scriptural version, "the truth shall make you free," nor the Comtean version, "science provides foresight and foresight provides the power to act" (which somehow sounds rather more compelling when translated back into French). Nor did they adopt the positivistic slogan set out by Friedrich Engels in his nominally antipositivistic tract, *Anti-Dühring*, when .

---

[15]Joseph J. Schwab has dealt with the "arts of Eclectic" in a series of evocative papers, among them: "The Practical Arts of Eclectic," *The School Review* 79 (August 1971), pp. 493–542; "What Do Scientists Do?" *Behavioral Sciences* 5 (January 1960), pp. 1–27.

he wrote of the "leap of mankind from the realm of necessity into the realm of freedom."

There are, in the reports on the Commissions, few signs of such assumptions. Instead, there are more than hints of concern with the basic and more modest question: Which forms of sociological and behavioral science knowledge made which kinds of difference to the recommendations adopted or rejected by the Commissions? In place of reveling in an orgy of unconnected facts, the researchers focused on strategic concepts and facts that sometimes affected the formulation of policy. Consider only these examples in Westoff's report on the Population Commission:

- *Item:* One study concluded that "population growth played a minor role in the short run" as demographic time is counted (thirty to fifty years) when "compared with technological, economic, and governmental policy considerations." Why did this broad factual conclusion prove to be strategic? Because it seemed to have an almost direct policy implication calling for specified contingency analysis and indicating that, *for the time being,* population control is a comparatively "indirect and ineffectual policy lever for environmental problems."

- *Item:* Another strategic finding was the demonstration that "if women averaged 2.0 rather than 2.1 births [and, of course, anyone can see that this minute average difference could scarcely matter], zero population growth could be achieved near the same level and in almost the same time with *immigration continued at the current volume.* Although not a world-shaking scientific discovery, this bit of demographic intelligence was extremely important in the debate over immigration policy and was influential in defeating a recommendation to reduce the volume."

These examples should not be taken to imply that there is typically a direct passage from sociological knowledge to social policy.[16] But to say

[16] In his review of this chapter, Irving Janis noted that the uses of pluralism could be formulated at this point in terms of the quality of the planning and decision-making process: the extensiveness of search; openness to a variety of kinds of relevant information concern-

more here about the gap between the two would only be redundant in view of Paul Lazarsfeld's close and informed analysis of the problem.

This brings us to a series of more detailed observations on the place of theoretical sociology in the research of the Commissions. These observations will take us somewhat afield to consider theoretical issues in the discipline at large which are implied in that research.

THEORETICAL ORIENTATIONS

A Focus on Consequences

Throughout much of their work, we are told, the Commissions focused on consequences: the consequences of existing practices and structures and the consequences anticipated from putting proposed policies into effect.

- *Charles Westoff:* The Population Commission "focused on the economic, environmental, political, and social consequences of population growth."
- *Otto Larsen:* The "fateful" decision was taken in the Congressional Act establishing the Commission on Pornography to adopt the position that "knowledge about *the effects* [i.e., the consequences] of exposure to explicit sex material [might be] relevant for making decisions about the forms of control that a society might exercise over obscenity."
- *Lloyd Ohlin:* "The most important inputs of social science knowledge to the Crime Commission were probably in the documentation of the harmful consequences of existing practices and policies and suggestions of a variety of persuasive theories and justifications for pursuing an alternative course."

The focus on consequences should come as no surprise to sociologists aware of the pervasive character of functional analysis in sociology, not least those sociologists busily engaged in repudiating that mode of analysis. After all, research bearing upon general policies dealing with socially

ing the consequences of proposed solutions; the range of possible solutions considered; alertness to contingencies that require special planning; and other factors. For an extensive analysis of decision-making in these terms, see Irving Janis and Leo Mann. *Decision Making: A Psychological Analysis of Conflict, Choice and Commitment.* (Forthcoming) defined problems in and of society *must* focus on multiple functional and dysfunctional consequences of alternative courses of action for a variety of social units (e.g., varied groups, strata, regions) and the more comprehensive social systems. This is the case even though no scientific calculus of course exists for assessing, choosing among, and integrating such diverse consequences.

The four Commissions can be thought of as having played out a scenario composed of tacit and explicit theoretical orientations calling for them to examine the probable outcomes of alternative policies. What produced and maintained the reported conflicts in the Commissions were principally the differences of interests, values, and ideologies affecting the weights to be assigned to selected consequences. So far as policy-oriented research is concerned, the critical conflict of interests and values centers on the question:

> Which evidence of which consequences for which social systems, strata, and groups should be taken into account in the research?

In all of the Commissions, the inescapable decision to select some, rather than other, expected consequences for investigation was basic to both the research program and the evolving rationale for alternative policies. To take only one instance, in the Population Commission it was this kind of value-charged, perspective-bound decision that divided the subgroup advocating the "unwanted fertility" perspective from the subgroup advocating the "ecological perspective."

Such conflicts highlight the untenable character of that long-forgotten positivism which, these days, is being revived by a small army of critics who promiscuously attribute caricatured versions of it to sociologists engaged in the empirical investigation of human problems in society. The research staffs of the Commissions evidently did not adopt the easygoing assumption that the sociological truth shall itself make it easy to choose among various courses of social action. Apart from much else, what makes such choices fundamentally underivable from sociological knowledge is the incommensurability of consequences that are in the interest of some sectors of the society and are dysfunctional for others. It is this basic feature of comprehensive decisions, most marked in a highly differentiated society, that leads to their inescapably acquiring a political character.

Thus, the overview of Presidential Commissions in action teaches us once again that when it comes to the formulation of public policy, one of the enduring problems facing sociologists is that of clarifying and working out some way of analyzing "the aggregate of humanly relevant consequences." That problem has long been on the agenda of a certain kind of functional and structural analysis.

What Harold Lasswell presciently, and in a sense prematurely, described as "the policy sciences" in the 1940s, referred chiefly to *social* research that is oriented to public and private policy.[17] Lasswell recognized that almost the entire spectrum of science could be drawn upon for investigations bearing upon the formation of policy, but he centered on the subset of the social sciences. Since his pioneering formulations, it has become possible to identify more of the distinctive contributions that social science can make to the formation of policy. Among these, I single out the sociological perspective that deals with latent social problems rather than with the manifest problem defined for investigation by the institutional powers that be.

Latent Social Problems

By latent social problems, I mean those unwanted social conditions that are at odds with some of the (often declared) values and interests of groups and strata in the society but are not generally recognized as being so. Sociologists do not impose their values upon others when they undertake to supply knowledge about latent problems that make them generally manifest. Thus, when demographers working for the Commission on Population, for example, try to identify the social, economic, and cultural consequences of various rates of population growth, they in effect call the advocates of differing population policies to account for the results of putting one or another policy into practice. The demonstrated consequences of uncontrolled birth rates, for example, can then be seen as the aggre-

[17]Daniel Lerner and Harold D. Lasswell, eds. *The Policy Sciences* (Stanford: Stanford University Press, 1951) provides an early summary of the Lasswellian perspective; Lasswell provides a more recent statement in *Pre-View of Policy Sciences* (New York: Elsevier, 1971). For most recent formulations of the field, see James F. Reynolds, "Policy Sciences: A Conceptual and Methodological Analysis." *Policy Sciences* 6 (1975), pp. 1–27; Laurence H. Tribe, "Policy Science: Analysis or Ideology?" *Philosophy and Public Affairs*, No. 2 (Fall, 1972) pp. 66–110; and Wehezkel Droer, *Design for Policy Sciences.* (New York: Elsevier, 1971).

gated result of people acting in accord with some of their values to produce outcomes that conflict with some of their other values.

This kind of latent social problem constitutes an important special case of the generic pattern of the unanticipated consequences of (individual or collective) social action.[18] Total commitments to values of every kind—whether these be the value set on rapid economic expansion ("growth"), rapid technologic advance, or rule-free communities or the value set on that full expression of self in which anything goes (analyzed by Lionel Trilling in the notion of "authenticity")—have cumulative consequences which, if not counteracted, in due course undercut the originating values themselves.

This sociological perspective turns up repeatedly in the research programs of the several Commissions. The same perspective is inherent in the newly popular intellectual and social movement known as technology assessment. In effect, technology assessment focuses on the latent consequences of actual or proposed technological developments. It is designed to search out previously unknown or unconsidered social, ecological, and other humanly relevant consequences of existing or proposed technological complexes.[19]

The implications of all this are significant for an evolving theory of policy-oriented social research because the emphasis upon discovering latent consequences of existing or contemplated arrangements, institutional or technological, puts the current sociological accent on the subjective component of social action in its appropriate context.

[18]The interest in unintended and unrecognized outcomes of social action has a long, discontinuous history from at least the time of Machiavelli, with contributions by such scholars as Vico, Adam Smith, Marx, Wundt, and to approach our own time, Pareto. The problematics is sketched out in R. K. Merton. "The Unanticipated Consequences of Purposive Social Action," *American Sociological Review*, 1936, Vol 1, pp. 894–904; is renewed and developed in the special case of "The Self-Fulfilling Prophecy," *The Antioch Review*, Summer 1948, pp. 193–210; is linked up with the concepts of "Manifest and Latent Functions" in *Social Theory and Social Structure* [1949] 1968; and is brought to bear on "latent social problems" in ibid., pp. 104ff and in R. K. Merton and R. A. Nisbet, eds. *Contemporary Social Problems* (New York: Harcourt Brace Jovanovich, 1971), pp. 806–7.

[19]A recent penetrating paper by one of the chief architects of a basic report on technology assessment can also serve as a root reference to the rapidly growing library on the subject: Laurence H. Tribe, "Technology Assessment and the Fourth Discontinuity: The Limits of Instrumental Rationality," *Southern California Law Review*, June 1973, Vol. 46, pp. 617–660.

Subjectivism

Emphasis upon the subjective component in social action has had a long history in sociology and an even longer history before we sociologists arrived on the historical scene. To choose not quite arbitrarily among the various versions emphasizing that subjective element, we call to mind the notion of *Verstehen* as advanced by Max Weber (and the many others influenced by him); Parsons's "voluntaristic theory of action"; Znaniecki's "humanistic coefficient"; MacIver's "dynamic assessment"; Schutz's "phenomenological perspective"; and that succinct memorable version expressed in the Thomas Theorem:

> If men define situations as real, they are real in their consequences.[20]

It is one thing to maintain, as was maintained by Weber and Thomas, among others, that the understanding of human action requires us to attend systematically to its subjective component. It is quite another thing to assume or maintain that action is *nothing but* subjective. That extravagance leads to sociological Berkeleyanism (the allusion is, of course, philosophical, not geographical). Total subjectivism conceives of social reality as consisting *only* in social definitions, perceptions, labels, assumptions, or ideas. A great injustice is visited upon W. I. Thomas whenever his theorem is thus exaggerated by being taken entirely out of context.

Exaggeration of a seminal truth produces its own brand of error. Total subjectivism, which maintains that only social definitions of the situation determine the character of human action and its consequences, manages to transform the Thomas Theorem into this fallacious maxim:

> If men do *not* define situations as real, they are not real in their consequences.

When the sufficient is thus transformed into the necessary, sociological error replaces sociological insight. This total subjectivism ignores the

---

[20]The Theorem appears once in the corpus of W. I. Thomas's writings: on page 572 of the book he wrote with Dorothy Swaine (Thomas) Thomas, entitled *The Child in America* (New York: Knopf, 1928).

objective constraints upon action—social, economic, technological, and other constraints—that are not caught up in social definitions. To ignore these constraints is to imply that they do not significantly affect consequences.

The theoretical hazard of total subjectivism did not first turn up in exaggerations of the recent labeling perspective on deviant behavior.[21] It was potentially there in any voluntaristic paradigm of action and was skirted by Parsons a quarter-century ago. Then, as now, the position taken on total subjectivism seemed to me fundamental to sociological theorizing:

> When Mr. Parsons notes that the "social situation" must be analyzed with respect to "the various types of significance of situational facts to the actor," there is need for further strict clarification. Does this mean that sociology takes into account *only* those aspects of the objective situation to which the acting individual [or group] is oriented (cognitively, affectively, or through goal-definitions)? Does it imply that observable aspects of the situation of which the acting individual [or group] is *wholly unaware* are at once eliminated from the realm of facts pertinent for the sociologist? If so, one must register dissent . . . it is all the more important to clarify this formulation, else one might suppose that he [Parsons] advocates a basically idealistic or subjectivistic approach to sociological theories, in which *only* those aspects of the situation somehow taken into account by individuals are considered pertinent to the sociological analysis.[22]

An adequate theoretical place can be provided for both individual

[21]As is often the case with the fate of ideas in the course of their diffusion, it is nr so much in the work of the principal initiators of the labeling perspective as in that of their epigoni that extreme subjectivism appears. The seminal works include: Edwin M. Lemert. *Human Deviance, Social Problems and Social Control* (Englewood Cliffs, N.J.: Prentice-Hall, 1967); Howard S. Becker. *The Outsiders,* (New York: (Free Press, 1973 second edition); Kai T. Erikson. "Notes on the Sociology of Deviance," *Social Problems,* 1962, Vol. 9, pp. 307–14 and *Wayward Puritans* (New York: John Wiley, 1966); J. I. Kitsuse, "Societal Reaction to Deviant Behavior," *Social Problems,* 1962, Vol. 9, pp. 247–56; A. V. Cicourel, *The Social Organization of Juvenile Justice* (New York: John Wiley, 1968). For a thoroughgoing critical review, see Edwin M. Schur. *Labeling Deviant Behavior: Its Sociological Implications* (New York: Harper & Row, 1971); Nanette J. Davis. "Labeling Theory in Deviance Research: A Critique and Reconsideration," *The Sociological Quarterly,* Fall 1972, Vol. 13, pp. 447–474.

[22]Robert K. Merton. "The Position of Sociological Theory," *American Sociological Review,* Vol. 13 (April 1948), p. 167.

and collective definitions of situations without adopting a wholly subjectiv-
istic position. As formulated in the concept of the self-fulfilling
prophecy,[23] collective definitions, shared by groups or collectives, make
up a significant *dynamic part of the social environment*. To the extent that
they are shared, subjective definitions become an *objective* part of that
environment, constraining the behavior both of people sharing the definitions and of people, also within the social system, rejecting them.

The research staffs of the Commissions have apparently avoided the
strong subjectivist imbalance that turns up in some sociological theorizing. To correct that imbalance and to restore the objective contexts of
action to their indispensable place, we plainly need this counterpart to
the Thomas Theorem:

> And if men do *not* define real situations as real, they are neverthe-
> less real in their consequences.

The paired theorems[24] serve as a continuing reminder of a truth that
the sociologist must acknowledge (despite the idiomatic expression to the
contrary): In society, as in other domains, what you don't know (or don't
notice) *can* hurt you.

Indeed, it is precisely what you do not know that will often hurt you
most, since you cannot take appropriate measures against the unknown.
Whether their causes were socially defined as real or not, tuberculosis
and Asiatic cholera managed to decimate many populations before Robert
Koch discovered their pathogenic agents and laid the basis for their control.

A major function, not only of research directly oriented toward public policy but of science generally, is to provide an improved understanding of socially induced situations that are *not* generally defined as real,
simply because of (sometimes motivated) ignorance. The geneticist
Joshua Lederberg has noted that it is ironic, but not surprising that
science comes to be penalized in the public estimation as the bearer of
evil tidings about the dysfunctional consequences of economically or cultur-

[23]Robert K. Merton, "The Self-fulfilling Prophecy," *The Antioch Review*, Summer
1948, pp. 193–210 (reprinted as Chapter 13 in *Social Theory and Social Structure, op. cit.*).

[24]As James March has pointed out on reading this proposed pairing, taken together
they plainly imply the simpler theorem: real situations have consequences. But, of course,
information is lost in the more general formulation.

ally preferred behaviors. Thus, as he recently observed, there may be

> some who wish we didn't know that radiation is mutagenic and
> carcinogenic. We could then use our atmosphere and other resources
> as sinks for our waste in that sphere, and get at least a short-term advan-
> tage of the economic utility of the procedures. Unfortunately, you can-
> not play those kinds of games with nature for very long. Those costs
> will be incurred to the extent that they are real . . . to the extent that
> there are actual health hazards . . . connected with them *whether you
> know about them or not*. Merely to be ignorant of them is simply to
> defer your recognition of them into the future—in no way to
> blunt . . . the actual impact.[25]

From the theoretical perspective being advanced here, it is of more
than passing interest to learn of the emphasis on the interplay between
subjective and objective aspects of the social reality found in the policy-
oriented research conducted for the four Commissions, which they variously used or ignored in arriving at their recommendations. Whatever
else requires change in the future programs of research for national commissions and other policy-formulating groups, such an orientation does
not.

CODA

The accounts by participant-connoisseurs of the national Commissions advance the continuing effort to clarify the character and workings of policy-
oriented sociological knowledge. They alert us to problems and prospects
that we may not have previously considered. Among these are implications for concerted research programs that might be mounted by the national and international communities of sociologists.

All four observers report a common circumstance confronting the
Commissions. In each sphere of inquiry, there was a conspicuously insufficient backlog of the needed social research. Some of the new research had
to be produced under forced draft; much of the rest could not be carried
through at all within the time available.

[25]Joshua Lederberg, in *A Tenth Anniversary Event: Remarks on the Tenth Anniversary of the National Institute of General Medical Sciences*, Washington: U.S. Department
of Health, Education and Welfare Publication No. (NIH) 74–274, 1974, p. 16.

This condition of *ad hoc* research under urgent pressure need not continue to be the typical condition. As sociologists attuned to structural and functional alternatives, we might remember that there really are other public institutions besides governmental ones. Among these are the composites of professional association and learned society—the American Sociological Association, for example, and many another of like kind. Perhaps these organizations should take it upon themselves, separately or in concert, to initiate continuing research programs designed for use by functional equivalents of governmental commissions. Independent commissions centered upon social problems on the grand scale could be instituted—say, by the Social Science Research Council—without regard to the immediacies of political expediency. They, in turn, could generate terms of reference for programs of policy-oriented research in the particular sphere of problem, without the strong pressures of urgency that have typically limited work done directly for Congressional and Presidential Commissions.

In a word, it is not really necessary to wait upon invitations from the White House or Congress to undertake continuing programs of policy-focused research of the kinds required by governmental commissions. Independent action by the community of social scientists in this domain would give added meaning to the social role of social science in the last quarter of our difficult century.

APPENDIX

To: The participants in the session on the role of sociologists in Presidential Commissions.

Subject: An analysis of your experience on a Presidential Commission.

From: Mirra Komarovsky

This discussion is not meant to be all-inclusive. It contains a set of questions that might become the starting point of each analysis and provide some common core of data. We have excluded statutory Congressional committees, White House conferences, and short-lived, fact-finding commissions because we assume that Presidential Commissions constitute a wide enough category for an initial investigation.

A study of Presidential Commissions may focus on two distinct problems: (1) the sociology of Presidential Commissions, or Presidential Commissions as a sociological phenomenon; and (2) the use of sociological concepts and research in Presidential Commissions (including non- and misuses).

The analysis should begin with the establishment of the Presidential Commission. Consider questions such as the following: Was the problem to be tackled by the commission a sudden crisis or one of long-standing duration? If the latter, what brought it to the forefront of public attention? What may be assumed to be the Presidential intention; A political gesture to assuage public unrest and to forestall action? To get support for a predetermined policy? To serve as an educational device to disseminate information? To seek expert advice and new ideas?

The inventory of the collectivities involved in the Presidential Commission may usefully usher in the organizational analysis. Most of the commissions include commissioners, an administrative staff, a research staff, perhaps a Presidential assistant, task forces, consultants, and witnesses. Other groups—governmental agencies, The White House, pressure groups, the mass media—may become involved at various stages.

The organizational analysis should contain as much data as possible on the method of selection of the personnal of these groups, the occupational composition of the personnel, the amount of time or the degree of involvement required in the work of the Commission, and the possible underrepresentation of groups having a manifest stake in the work of the Commission. These matters may have implications not only for intergroup relationships during the life of the commission, but for the nature of the final recommendations and the concern with the implementation of the results once the report is submitted. For example, if the composition is bipartisan and bicameral (Senate and House) with representatives of various interest groups, the pressure for consensus may result in inoffensive, but trivial, recommendations.

In the scrutiny of the strains inevitably arising in the deliberations of the Presidential Commissions, consider the hypotheses presented by Robert K. Merton concerning problems of communication between various professions and between policy-makers and intellectuals.[1] Merton's discussion is also relevant to other sections of this memorandum.

Another example of possible conflict may be a struggle between competing permanent governmental agencies who may feel threatened and therefore attempt to influence the recommendations in their favor. The role of the executive director should be studied, since it is he who tends to be the mediator between commissioners and research staff.

Turning to the original charge to the Commission, how would you evaluate it with regard to open-endedness? Two polar possibilities suggest themselves. The charge may be so stated as to force the sociologists into the role of technicians (to use Merton's term) assigned to buttress a predetermined program or policy. At the other extreme, the original formulation may have been too diffuse and in need of focus.

[1] Robert K. Merton, *Social Theory and Social Structure* (New York: The Free Press, 1968), pp. 261–268.

Is it possible to trace the process of reformulation of the original charge? Did it become increasingly clear that certain assumptions were frozen and that the commission was expected to produce support for a previously established policy? How much leeway was provided for alternative statements of the nature of the problem? What were the independent variables affecting the early course of this reformulation: A directive from the White House? A premature leak to Congress or to the mass media? The political influence of certain commissioners?

Did the sociologist have the knowledge to reformulate the nature of the problem in a more productive way? Did his failure to do so stem from the lack of political influence to overcome resistance? For example, the problem as defined by the commission may have been known to the sociologist as a symptom bound to persist unless more fundamental changes were made. Similar issues arise with regard to recommendation.

In examining the final recommendations of the commission, it might be useful to begin with the frustrations that you, as sociologist, have experienced. Were the frustrations caused by nonexistence of valid sociological knowledge relevant to the policy issues in question? Or, was the existing knowledge unacceptable to politically more powerful groups on the Commission? Undoubtedly, the problem of the uses and nonuses of sociological knowledge is more complex than these stark alternatives.

The relative failure of the sociologist to make the maximum contribution may be attributed to some of the following:

1 Lack of familiarity with the technical features of the institutional context within which the problem is located (e.g., administration of criminal justice, hospitals, economic enterprises).

2 Any single discipline, including sociology, selects certain aspects of reality at the expense of others. A sociological generalization, therefore, carries the implicit clause: "other conditions being equal." But the policy-maker, operating in the real world, is obliged to take into account a wider range of relevant variables.

3 The scarcity of funds or time to supply answers to problems of policy options when primary research is impossible.

4 The scarcity of research directed specifically towards issues of current social concern. The need exists for systematic re-

search, evaluating the effectiveness of delivered services on various dimensions as well as innovating experimental research.

Could one design, were time and finances available, research that would furnish a scientific basis for the commission's recommendations? Research could specify what value choices were made and at what costs/benefits to particular groups of the population. Nevertheless, a gap between research and social policy is inevitable. An outcome of a policy in a complex and changing society (however grounded in research) would be, at best, a probabalistic prediction.

We have discussed the limitations in the current state of sociological knowledge. But participants on a given commission may have felt unable to incorporate whatever knowledge sociologists do possess. One way to tackle this question is to ask: "In what ways would the recommendations have differed had sociologists been solely responsible for writing the final report?" A strictly sociological set of recommendations might have differed from the actual report because of the ideological and value commitments characteristic of sociologists, which are in contrast to other more politically powerful constituencies of the commission. Would the characteristic input of sociologists derive from the general sociological orientation, the knowledge of institutional interrelationships and the recognition of the utopian nature of proposals, given the perpetuation of certain conditions?

Another type of sociological input differs from the preceding varieties. A proposed "remedy" for the problems in question may be based upon an intuitive assessment of a variety of relevant conditions, their potential for change and the ensuing consequences. A truly innovative judgment of this sort may emerge as a social invention (e.g., Federal Insurance of Savings Deposits, Regional Authorities). The accumulated sociological expertise in a given problem area may enable the sociologist to make such an assessment more readily than could an administrator or other specialists. Finally, although we have remarked upon the scarcity of such research, it is conceivable that no matter how firmly grounded in a scientific data a given recommenddation was, the commission rejected it on political or ideological grounds.

Yet some resistance to such input of the sociologists might have been forestalled by a more sophisticated knowledge of politics, of governmental bureaucracies, by a more deliberate education of other collectivities on the Commission, by a different handling of mass media, or by other tactics.

You will have considered up to this point the various difficulties experienced by the sociologists caused by the lack of relevant data or by the political obstacles to the utilization of existing data. But consider the contributions that the sociologists did make to the final report. It would be useful to specify these contributions at various stages of the commission's work, from possible redefinition of the original charge to final recommendations.

The last section of the analysis should deal with the aftermath and the consequences of the commission's work. The immediate and the long-range effects may be distinguished. If the commission had no effect on public policy, what accounted for this failure: Opposition of the President? No organization to carry on the political struggle for implementation? A decline in the public interest in the issue?

The immediate or long-range social effects of the Commission may include a social invention; and the confrontation of conflicting interest groups within the Commission may have resulted in some mutual concessions. Consider also the evidence of heightened public awareness of the actual extent or causes of problems leading, in turn, to shifts in public opinion more favorable to certain programs.